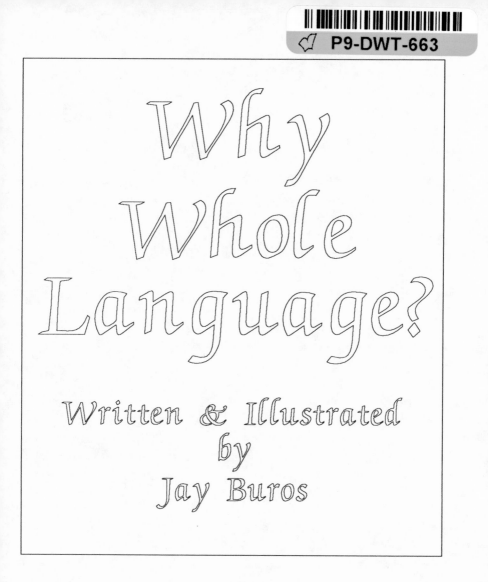

Why Whole Language?

Written & Illustrated
by
Jay Buros

PUBLISHED BY
MODERN LEARNING PRESS
ROSEMONT, NEW JERSEY

WHY
· WHOLE ·
LANGUAGE?

by
Jay Buros

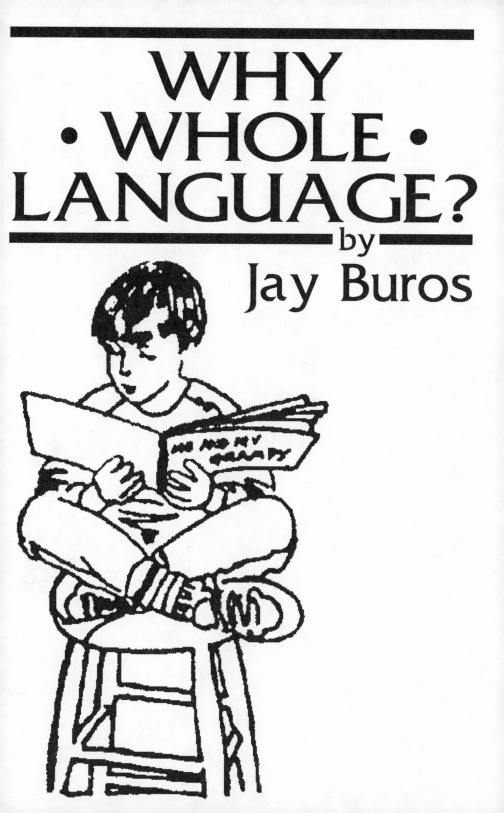

Dedicated to
MOM, DAD
JOANIE and FRANK

Acknowledgements

Many supportive people contributed to the process that culminated in the creation of this book.

My family, especially my mother and father, were my first and most important teachers. We were encircled by wonderful aunts and uncles called the "Greats" because they are!

In New Hampshire, Ben Haubrich helped me find the time, energy and commitment to teach in a caring way. Kathy Matthews, Barbara Linder and other members of the New Hampshire Association of Readiness Teachers helped me get started with Whole Language -- especially Sharon Cadieux, who gave me my first Big Book. I would also like to thank the members of the TAWL (Teachers Applying Whole Language) groups who shared their experiences and wisdom with me.

At the Jaffrey-Peterborough School District, Ken Greenbaum, Moe LeFlem, Bob Reidy, and Larry Bramblett provided vital leadership and support for implementing the reading and writing process. Paula Fleming provided motivation and guidance for all the teachers, and for me especially as I began to do my first Whole Language workshops.

As a workshop leader and consultant, I have received ongoing support from Bill Page, John Poeton, Jean Mann, Diana Mazzuchi, Nancy Richard, Linda Pass, Bob Johnson, Jim Grant and many fellow professionals who are helping teachers understand and implement the Whole Language approach.

As to this book, Robert Low has helped guide my hand and supported me all the way. Bert Shapiro encouraged me to do the illustrations and so started me on a new, exciting path. Diane Taylor and Valerie Pietraszewska assisted me in the actual sketching by showing me the "how's."

I thank you all, and especially the children, parents and dedicated classroom teachers who have so enriched my life.

Contents

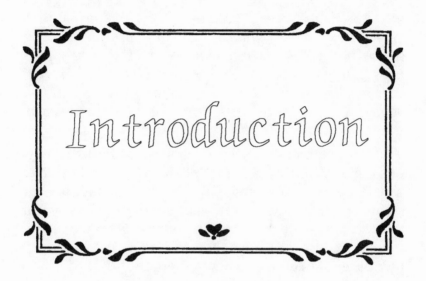

Introduction

When I was in elementary school, I had great difficulty spelling. My papers were returned to me covered with red marks, which made me feel ashamed and "not good" at writing. Naturally, I didn't like to write. Decades later, I still feel reluctant to write and to show my writing to others.

*Reading was not my strong point, either. (I was "good" at art, sports, and talking with friends.) Books never really interested me until one summer when I was helping my mother clean out my grandmother's basement. My mother showed me one of her favorite childhood books, **Keeper of the Bees** by Jean Stratton Porter. I began reading it and loved it, suddenly discovering how exciting reading could be. At that point, I was already in junior high school, but from then on reading was a favorite activity and opened many doors.*

Every elementary school teacher has had students like me, and many teachers probably were students like me. We now know that initial learning experiences create attitudes in children --about learning and about themselves -- which can last a lifetime. Negative experiences and the attitudes they create can be overcome, but rather than allowing new generations of students to develop negative attitudes about reading and writing, many teachers have started using new teaching methods which make learning to write a positive experience, and which help children experience the joys of reading right when they are learning to read. These new teaching methods, which have strong roots in the past, are now known as Whole Language.

When I first began exploring this approach, Whole Language was not the widely publicized phenomenon it has since become. Like many other teachers, I was drawn to the Whole Language approach because it made sense to me, based on my own experiences as a student and a teacher. And, like many other educators, I continued to develop and use Whole Language techniques because I saw that they worked in the classroom, helping children learn and enjoy the process.

The Whole Language approach also helped me develop as a teacher and as a person. It allowed me to be more creative in the classroom, and to build more positive relationships with students. The integration of other subjects within the Whole Language approach also resulted in my developing new interests which had not been meaningful to me in the past. As I helped my students study things that interested them, such as birds, flowers and star formations, I learned more about nature than I did in 16 years of formal schooling. And, I learned that all children are natural scientists; all we need to do is help them study what interests them.

In recent years, I've conducted many workshops on Whole Language, and I've seen many teachers go through similar transformations. As they begin to implement their own versions of the Whole Language approach and see it work in their classrooms, they often develop more positive attitudes about teaching and discover new interests and capabilities of their own. When we learn from our students as well as teach them, we also learn more about ourselves.

Now that this former student who wasn't good at writing has written a book about learning to read and write, one part of the process has come full circle for me. I'm sure many of my former teachers would be amazed to learn that I've written a book, especially about this subject. At times, I'm still amazed, too, but I'll never feel that way about my former students. Most of them became "published" and "celebrated" authors during their first years of school, so they and I know they have the ability and the talent to be good writers, as well as good readers.

Our greatest responsibility and challenge as teachers is to help our students experience success in our classrooms every day. I hope this book will make it easier for that to happen, and allow everyone to enjoy the process.

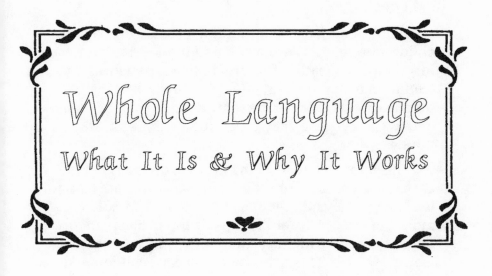

Whole Language
What It Is & Why It Works

When I talk with a group of adults, I often ask "How many of you like to write?" Very few -- maybe 10% -- raise their hands. When I ask the others why they don't like to write, many of them say they were "turned off" to writing at an early age by criticism of their handwriting or their spelling or their ideas. And, they say the critics who turned them off were their teachers.

Whole Language is a natural process of teaching children to read, write, speak and think -- by immersing them in meaningful, "real-life" experiences that lead to personal fulfillment. It's a way of helping children learn and enjoy at the same time, so that they read and write because they want to, as children and as adults.

This approach to teaching is based on the belief that each child has a natural desire to learn, an individual learning style, and creative abilities. As a Whole Language teacher, I carefully observe and listen to students, in order to identify their individual interests and learning styles. This helps me teach each child in ways that involve his or her interests, strengths and creativity.

I also view the process of learning to read and write as an extension of learning to listen and talk. So, I use some of the same techniques parents use, in order to build on my students' initial success in learning to communicate. I demonstrate what I want the children to do, so that they can see and hear what is expected, and then imitate me. I accept and encourage approximations as an important part of this learning process, just as parents do when children are saying their first words. And, like a parent, I try to establish a safe and caring environment, in order to support the risk-taking needed for growth, without jeopardizing the feelings of success and self-esteem that each child needs.

In a Whole Language classroom, children learn to read and write by reading and writing what interests them, with the support and guidance of the teacher. The emphasis is on learning by doing. This active involvement culminates in students creating their own books, which gives them a sense of pride and owner-ship in regard to what they have learned. Rather than just copying from a chalkboard or filling in worksheets, the children become authors while they are still in the primary grades.

In addition, learning to read and write is combined with other activities in a Whole Language classroom, so that students are not forced to learn skills which seem abstract and unrelated. Learning occurs within a "mean-ingful context," so that students have an interest in the subject matter and a desire to acquire new skills that further their interest.

A more detailed exploration of the Whole Language approach appears in later chapters. At this point, I want to provide an overview of the most important aspects, so you, the reader, can also learn about the various elements within the context of the larger whole.

Thinking

While we all want children to think, common practices at home and at school tend to discourage this activity. At home, many children are left in front in the television for hours every day, which forces them to learn passively, if at all. Many children are also provided with limited opportunities to play, or they have much of their play directed by parents, and as play is the primary means of learning for young children, these trends also inhibit the development of children's thought processes.

At school, the reliance on workbooks in the early primary grades has a similar effect. Using a workbook is like taking a test every day. There's only one right answer for each question, and the students are forced to follow an inflexible, repetitive procedure within a limited time frame. This pressures young children to think in a limited and unnatural way, rather than taking time to explore their interests, discover new possibilities, and consider a wide range of options.

Whole Language encourages children to think by making choice and risk-taking part of the learning experience. When children can decide what they want to write about, instead of simply filling in a blank, they learn to think for themselves and make decisions. They also feel safer working this way, because they will be not be rewarded only for the "right" answer and penalized for everything else. Even when mistakes are made, the mistakes are accepted as an instructive part of the learning process, rather than viewed as personal and academic failures.

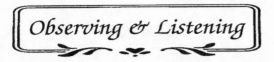

Observing & Listening

These skills are crucial elements of the learning process and most adult activities. Yet many schools simply assume that children know how to listen and observe, with no further help or instruction needed. At the same time, frequent television watching exerts a strong influence on how children observe and listen, accustoming them to brief, dazzling presentations and frequent changes of topic, thereby creating expectations which are not met by real-world situations.

Whole Language helps children become effective observers and listeners. By respecting a child's individual learning process, a Whole Language teacher encourages the use of the senses and the intellect, then helps the child communicate his or her feelings and thoughts.

In a Whole Language classroom, children focus on objects of interest, write descriptions of them, and draw them. Similarly, the use of music, drama and art helps children appreciate new and different ways words can be used. The children are also encouraged to learn from each other by observing and listening. And, the children can imitate a teacher who acts as a role model by observing students, listening to them, and writing about them.

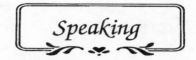

Speaking

In many American classrooms, children rarely speak. The teacher does the talking, and the children are expected to sit quietly until called upon. (I'm sure you know how well they do that.) When the teacher asks a question, the children raise their hands, often in silent competition to be chosen by the almighty teacher. A child who wants to learn from another child or discuss a new discovery is likely to be punished for talking out of turn. The natural inclination to communicate is therefore discouraged.

In a Whole Language classroom, there are a few times when everyone is silent, but mostly there is a low hum as children communicate and learn with each other. Respecting children's natural learning process means recognizing that children love to talk, need to talk, and therefore should talk. Rather than interfering with learning, this can be an informative and enjoyable part of the process.

Given the opportunity, children will gladly teach each other and learn from each other. In fact, children can often teach other children more effectively than an adult can. And, this sort of interaction frees the teacher to work individually with different students, or to observe how children are interacting, in order to understand them better and individualize the curriculum accordingly.

Writing

Many schools fail to recognize the difference between the process of writing and the skills of spelling and penmanship. Writing is an act of communication, or at least self-expression; penmanship and spelling are skills that contribute to the process. A child who wants to write will learn spelling and penmanship; a child whose initial interest in writing is discouraged because of spelling or penmanship will have little interest in writing, spelling or penmanship.

Whole Language recognizes that using approximations of both letters and words is a natural part of the learning process, as is the use of pictures. It helps children progress through the phases of learning to write by providing encouragement and recognition, so that the children retain their self-esteem and motivation to learn.

The creation of books from children's writing is an important part of this process. It confirms the value of their efforts and provides a sense of ownership in a most tangible way. When the children illustrate the covers of their books, practice reading them, and present them to a larger audience during an Authors' Tea, the pride and enjoyment they feel is "written" all over their faces.

For generations of Americans, learning to read at school meant books about Dick and Jane and their dog, Spot. Initial reading experiences often were limited to sentences like "See Spot run up the hill." Not surprisingly, many of these same Americans have had little interest in reading as students and adults, far preferring electronic media like television and videos, which they think are more exciting than books.

Whole Language exposes children to a wide range of literature, so that they understand the variety of exciting experiences reading can provide. Picture books, children's literature, poems, songs, magazines and other printed materials are essential elements of a Whole Language classroom. So are the recently developed publications known as "Big Books," which have a large and colorful format designed to meet the needs of beginning readers. These sorts of materials help children learn to read and develop a life long love of books.

Whole Language teachers read to children every day and provide time for children to practice reading by themselves or with each other. The children are also allowed to select what they want to read, so that reading is interesting and meaningful to them. A child who does not relate to Dick, Jane and Spot may be fascinated by a book about dinosaurs or airplanes or an ugly duckling. This sort of experience can provide the motivation for continued learning, with new skills being acquired to further the child's interest, rather than because the teacher said so.

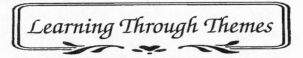

Learning Through Themes

Traditionally, subjects like reading, science, art, and math have been considered separate fields. They were taught in different ways at different times of the day. Links between the subjects sometimes occurred but were not viewed as particularly important.

Whole Language provides opportunities for children to learn about various subjects in an integrated way. The use of themes over a week or more allows indepth exploration of topics that naturally involve a variety of disciplines. For example, an integrated dinosaur theme lets children read about dinosaurs, draw dinosaurs, count and classify dinosaurs, visit a museum, write about dinosaurs, and even create their own dinosaur book. As part of this process, they might also learn about fossils and archeology, the history of the earth, and the structure of animals' bodies.

Learning in this way is a more meaningful experience for children, because the different skills and information they acquire are part of a broader interest and have a purpose. Just as many adults would be reluctant to learn new skills or information unless there was a reason for it, children also need to understand how they can use what they are learning.

Sharing

Most adults were educated in classrooms where the teacher did all the teaching and the students did all the learning. The roles were clear and distinctly different. But, if a teacher had little to teach or did not teach well, most students did not learn very much.

In addition to working together informally, children in a Whole Language classroom have organized opportunities to share their thoughts and feelings. When a student has been reading to a group or showing some work or sharing something from home, other children have an opportunity to respond, and the student who did the work gets to choose who will respond. This helps build everyone's self-esteem, as the students actually teach and support each other, which they usually love to do.

Whole Language recognizes that children naturally learn from each other by collaborating. When they share information or projects with each other, they're giving each other ideas, acting as role models, and supporting each other's development. They're also learning the social skills needed to work in any sort of organization.

As a Whole Language teacher, I still need to provide information, support, and direction, as well as to recognize and meet individual needs. But I also know that children who find learning to be an interactive, cooperative social experience -- rather than a solitary, passive one -- are likely to learn more, enjoy the process, and develop an active interest in it.

Child-Centered Teaching

Traditional teaching methods forced students to pay attention to the teacher, but they did not require the teacher to consider the interests of each student. Only those students who were very good or very bad received much individual attention. The teacher was more like a boss who decided what the entire class should learn and how they should learn it -- in essence, who the children should be.

A Whole Language teacher studies and learns from students, so that any instruction can be as individualized and effective as possible. A Whole Language teacher also provides many opportunities for students to choose what they want to learn and how they want to learn it, so that the teacher can learn more about the students, and the children can develop decision making abilities, initiative, and self-esteem. Children are treated and respected as individuals, and they tend to have fewer academic and discipline problems as a result.

Why Whole Language? It's a natural process that motivates children to learn to read and write, by encouraging them to read and write every day about topics that interest them. It respects children's developmental needs and keeps them actively involved in the learning process. It also helps students pursue their interests, learn from each other, use a wide range of skills, and take pride in what they've accomplished.

Why Whole Language? It makes learning enjoyable and interesting, and it works.

The Whole
Language Learning
Experience

I was warned about a student named Mark before I ever met him. His parents said he tried to burn down the house, fought with his brothers and sisters, and deliberately banged his head against the wall. When Mark started school, I just watched him at first, and I soon saw that he was an incredible artist who could also make just about anything.

One of the things Mark made was a typewriter with keys on it. He did not know any of the letters of the alphabet at the beginning of the year, but after playing on the typewriter, he put all the letters on the keys, and eventually he knew all those letters. He also began working on art projects at school, and he did so well that the other children began consulting him about their ideas. He became the "expert," which helped him develop the confidence and skills needed to read and write, too.

As so often happens, Mark's learning to read and write grew out of a wide variety of activities and interests, not just reading and writing instruction. Mark had talent, and once that talent was identified and supported, it could help Mark with reading, writing, math, science or any other subject. It also helped him develop a much more positive attitude about life and shine in school, rather than hurt himself or anyone else.

I believe that every child is talented, and an important part of my job is to discover those talents. Once I've done that, I can do more to help each student develop his or her capabilities.

This approach allows children to flourish in a Whole Language classroom, and it makes learning to read and write a natural part of the growth process. It also means that many aspects of the school day are part of the Whole Language curriculum. This chapter therefore looks at a wide spectrum of influences and activities which are part of the Whole Language approach.

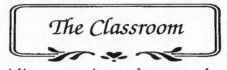

The Classroom

By providing a variety of areas where different activities can take place, the classroom design can help children discover and explore their diverse talents. I like to have an area for writing supplies, a math area, a library, a listening post, an art area, a drama area, and for young children, a sand table or water table and a block area.

In addition, there should be an open area where the students can gather as a group, either sitting on a rug or on chairs. This area is particularly important because it enables each child to share Whole Language experiences with the entire class.

Instead of individual desks, which limit and isolate the children, tables help children work together in small groups. And, when children can sit any where they want, they can follow their interests and I can learn more about their individual learning styles.

However, organization is also a must in a Whole Language classroom, and too much open space is difficult for children. Space that encourages them to flow from experience to experience works much better.

As children enter the classroom, they have buckets or washtubs for their personal belongings. They also have a writing area or tray with all their writing implements and supplies in it.

This layout allows the children to pick up their writing materials as soon as writing begins. They can then take the materials wherever they want to go and start work right away. And, in addition to their own materials, a writing supplies area should have extra pencils and markers, a stamp pad, masking tape, staplers, blank books and loose blank paper children can use to make their own books. A place to display books they have made is also very important.

In another area of the room, the children have folders they use to keep track of their reading. I help with the record keeping when children are young, but older children can keep records for themselves.

As to the classroom library, it should have a wide variety of books, not just those geared to the students' age level. Besides great literature, a good Whole Language library has joke books, picture books, poetry books, biographies, and guides to different plants, animals and regions. Even catalogs can stimulate children's interest in reading. And, having the publications' front covers showing makes the children more likely to read them.

Flannel board stories and magnetic stories are also very popular, because they let children participate in telling the story. Some children like to use pointers when they read, so it's good to have a container of those on hand. Pencils with little things like dinosaurs on one end seem to work particularly well as pointers.

Bulletin boards are another important element in the Whole Language environment, because they help to surround the children with meaningful print. Placing them at the children's height makes them easier to read, and covering the bulletin board with fabric makes the background more colorful.

Items that might appear on a bulletin board include the daily calendar, a "good morning" song, a weather chart, and a birthday chart. The jobs and responsibilities for the week should appear there, along with as much other record keeping as possible. (Children like to see how records are kept.) And, of course, each child's work should be displayed on a bulletin board at one time or another.

In addition, one bulletin board area can be devoted to "The Special Person of the Week." At the beginning of the year, I put all the children's names into a hat, along with my name, the principal's name, and the names of other educators who work with the children. Each week, we pull out one name, and then the child or I write the person's name on the bulletin board along a list of the person's favorite things -- my favorite breakfast, my favorite book, my favorite song, my favorite movie, my favorite actor, etc. A photograph on the bulletin board also helps make a child who is chosen feel special, as does a note from a parent or sibling. (In addition, we also put together a book in which everyone writes about the child and why he or she is special. The child makes the cover for it, we dedicate it to the child with love, and it becomes his or her special book.)

Another important component of classroom organization is making sure that all the materials in the room have their own storage places, labeled with their pictures and written names. Children keep the room in order when everything has a "home." The storage places should also be within reach of the students, so that all the materials are accessible to all the students and they feel it's their room.

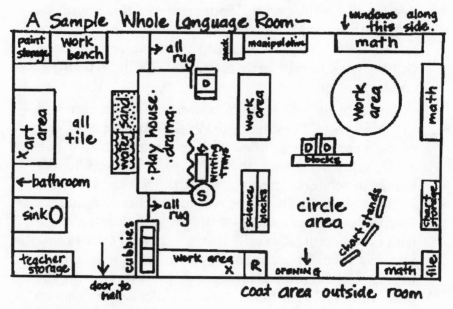

A Sample Whole Language Room —

D = DESK
S = SUPPLIES ··· WRITING
X = LISTENING POST
R = RECORD PLAYER

The Daily Schedule

Consistency provides safety, both for children and for teachers. A daily schedule helps to create a structured environment in which children feel free to focus on their interests.

At the same time, flexibility is also a necessity, whether for carefully prepared special events or a spontaneous learning experience. Balancing the need for consistency and flexibility may not be easy, but it is an important part of teaching.

The schedule I use works well for me and my students, so I'll briefly describe it here. However, other teachers may find a different approach works better for them. The components of the schedule are what matter most, so they are described in more detail in the sections that follow this one.

At nine o'clock, school begins. As soon as the children arrive, I like to have an opening routine during which we sing, update the calendar, and review anything else that's new on the front bulletin board. Then they go off to art, music or gym. This might seem disruptive, but it actually works better than having the children leave at later, arbitrary times like 1:45 on Tuesday and 2:15 on Thursday. Children adapt better if they know when to expect something, and a consistent, understandable schedule is particularly important when students are still learning to tell time.

On Thursday mornings, all the children in the entire school meet in the gym for a school meeting with the principal, who is assisted by the art, music and gym teachers. There, the children learn about safety, meet policemen and other local officials, and "share" as a school-wide community. It's a great time for a sing-along session.

At the same time, the classroom teachers have a "team meeting," early childhood meeting, or whatever. This gives the teachers time to interact as professionals -- coordinating with each other and learning from each other -- before they become involved with the children. Trying to do the same thing after school is much more difficult, because everyone is tired from the busy school day and has other things to do.

After the children return to the classroom, we have a sharing session, which is followed by a snack. Early in the fall, we go outside for recess after snack time, but when the cold weather starts in November, we stay inside for what I call "noisy reading." A writing period comes next, followed by lunch, and then we have a Whole Language reading period which may also be integrated with other subjects. After that, the children are growing tired and I am, too, so we wind up with a free choice period and then everyone goes home.

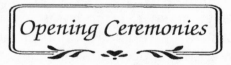

Opening Ceremonies

The children and I like to start the school day with an exciting "good morning" song to wake us all up. ("Good Morning" and "It's A Beautiful Day" from the record set called **We All Live Together** work particularly well. The records also contain many other great songs; more information about them is available in the Appendix.) The children all come to know and love these songs during the first few months of school.

We then sing the days of the week, and we start finding out what today is and what tomorrow will be. The calendar helps us name the day of the week, the month, and the date. This information is put in a "Today is..." chart, and we also use an "odd/even" chart to figure out if the date is an odd or even number. (This technique and the one that follows are derived from Mary Baratta-Lorton's *Mathematics Their Way*, which is also referenced in the Appendix.)

For another part of our opening ceremonies, I use a roll of tape from an adding machine to help us keep track of how many days of school we've had. On the first day of school, I write the numeral 1 at the start of the roll. On the second day, I write a 2, continuing the process each day until we reach 100. On the hundredth day, we have a celebration, which includes counting groups of 100 or more specially collected items such as buttons, blocks, stickers, and pencils. Eventually, the children will see that we are in school together for 180 days, and they practice counting by 2's, 5's, and 10's to 180.

On Mondays, the opening ceremonies include my asking the children which jobs they would like for the week. Among the choices are King or Queen (we have a King or Queen chair), Line Leader, Milk Helpers, Door Holder, Plant Waterer, and Attendance Taker. Records of who has done which job are kept right in front of the children, so they understand how I try to be

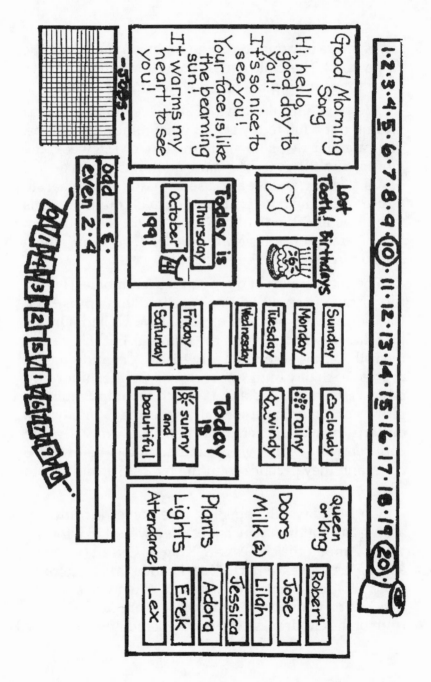

fair.That makes a big difference, and children love to know the teacher's system.

Sometimes, I also write a note to the class using large print on a big piece of white paper. If someone is having a birthday or other special event, I usually include something about that. Then I ask the children to try to figure out what I've written, and it's like a game or a puzzle for them. Most of the time, they succeed because the message has meaning for them, and reading becomes fun! (This is especially true when there are names in the message -- children love to see their names in print.)

By January, the students have learned a great deal about the written language, so every morning before they arrive I put up chart paper with the "daily news" on it. Sometimes, I write each sentence in a different color, so students can more easily see what a sentence is. Or, I may cover one word to see if they can use the context to figure out what word it is.

The chart can then be reviewed with the entire class, and the children asked to read it aloud together. You can also ask them what they can tell you about rhyming words, beginning sounds, endings, spelling rules, punctuation, etc. And, because the messages on the chart are personally meaningful to them, the children are more inclined to absorb the lessons that can be derived from this sort of work.

We also use words from the chart to play a game called Rocketship, which is similar to a game that was called Hangman when I was growing up. (I changed the name and picture used because I didn't like the old image.) I draw a number of blank lines which correspond to the letters of a word, and as they guess the letters and the word, I fill in the blanks. This process focuses their attention on the number of letters in a word, the beginning and ending sounds, and the vowels and consonants. I also draw part of a rocketship each time they guess a letter, and they get a certain number of points each time they complete a word. The game puts them in competition with me, which helps them pay attention, but in the end, they always win. Once they have 100 points, everyone gets a special treat.

Sharing

Sharing is a whole-class activity, similar to what used to be called "show and tell," in which individual students present objects or tell stories to the rest of the class. It is important to have all the children participate, but I found that if too many children present things on the same day, everyone has to sit still for too long, and some children start to lose interest or act out. So, four or five children do the presenting each day of the week, and their day to share usually stays the same throughout the year.

Rather than have the children bring in toys or other commercial products from home for sharing, I suggest to the children and their parents (at the first parent meeting) that they bring in something that other children can learn from, possibly even something the parent and child did together. The parent is also invited to watch the child share, because often parents learn that a child is very different in school or in front of a group. I also make a point of saying that the children should participate in the decision as to whether or when the parents watch.

During sharing sessions, all the children sit on chairs, which are arranged in a circle. As chairs tend to be more comfortable than sitting on the floor, they help keep the children from growing distracted.

The children who do the presenting are "teaching" their peers, so I ask them to try to teach three things during each session at the start of the year, five things by December, seven by March, and up to ten by May. This really should vary as to how the children are developing, however. Some have lots to say naturally, so I just let them go, but those who have less to say should not be pressured to keep up with the more vocal ones.

Another technique that works well is to let a few children respond to the person who has been sharing. This makes the process more valuable for everyone by increasing the amount of active participation and feedback. Those who want to respond raise their hands, myself included, and the person who has done the sharing chooses three respondents. In addition to empowering the children, this provides information about how they relate to others, including myself. If I am always ignored by a student, it shows that I need to work harder on our relationship.

To give just a few examples of sharing, Daniel had made up a song about a puppy with his Mom, and he brought in a keyboard with a memory which he used to play it for us. With his permission, we made a chart of the song, so it became a means of learning about writing and reading, as well.

Tasha wrote a beautiful piece of poetry, and when I asked if we could make a chart of it, she said she wanted to illustrate it. So, we made the chart, and then she illustrated it, signed it, and dated it. It became part of our reading lesson throughout the year, and it taught me how much children like to illustrate, sign, and date their work.

One day Adora brought in her ballet costume and her Swan Lake record, in order to perform a dance for all of us. It showed everyone a new, special side of her. Brian shared an entire game he had invented, with his own home-made pieces and rules. Eric brought in his bunny, and Robert brought in his new baby brother (with help from Mom).

In response, the other children made comments such as:

"Robert, thank you for sharing your baby brother."
"Robert, your baby brother feels soft."
"Robert, you're my very best friend."

The last comment tends to be repeated again and again, because children love to share and to support each other. In addition to the fun it provides, this process is a valuable opportunity for students to observe, learn, discuss, and then write about things that are important to them. It also teaches me a great deal about the students, making me a more effective teacher.

And, the link between home and school is strengthened by the sharing process, which makes learning all the more meaningful for the children.

Noisy Reading

Noisy reading began as "sustained silent reading". By adapting the concept to the children, instead of the other way around, it became noisy reading because that's the way so many young children actually learn to read. (Some children still need time to read aloud when they are in third grade.)

The basic idea is that children learn to read by reading. This may sound obvious, yet studies have shown that children who are learning to read spend an average of less than five minutes per day reading, nationwide. And, much of that time is required reading for answering workbook questions or passing a test, which often makes it an anxiety-ridden task instead of an enjoyable experience.

On the first day of noisy reading, I let the children choose any book they want and as many books as they want. Some might read five books in one day, while others might take two weeks to read one book. Children can choose books (including picture books and books written by other children), magazines, flannel board stories, reading charts, or catalogs, to name just a few possibilities. They can be alone or with anyone they choose, as long as they are reading or looking at pictures.

Early in the year, noisy reading lasts about five to seven minutes, but by June it's up to about twenty minutes. From time to time, children talk about books they liked or didn't like, and that naturally inspires everyone to read even more. It also helps me learn more about the children and suggest other books they might want to consider.

Another important aspect of noisy reading is record keeping. I make a typed list of all the books in the classroom and photocopy it, so I have one in each child's reading folder. Then when a child reads to me, I highlight the title on that child's list. I also use codes to record how they are reading -- whether they are relying on memory, or are emergent readers, and so on. (I use codes only because they are quick and easy; I don't have time for anything more complex.) Once children reach first grade, they can start keeping their own reading lists, which involves them even more in the learning process.

Writing Process

Writing follows noisy reading, and in this activity too, choice is an important means of involving children in the learning process. Equally important are accepting the children as they are and gently encouraging them to take risks, so that they feel comfortable as well as involved.

The writing process starts on the first day of school, when each child chooses which color tray they want. I write each child's name on his or her tray, and do the same with the box of crayons and the pencil that each child receives. I also create a folder labeled "Things I Know" for each child, so we can keep track of the progress being made, and of course, that has the child's name on it, too. This way the children keep all their writing materials together and available in their trays, and the value of being able to write is reinforced by the sense of ownership which comes with having their name identify their possessions.

During the daily writing period, children are free to draw or write whatever they want, at their own rate. I move among the children, squatting beside them or sitting in a small chair, to observe and to offer assistance if they want it. Here are some examples of the sorts of activities that take place during writing time early in the school year:

Christopher is drawing a picture, and when I ask him to tell me about it, he says it's a picture of the sun, a house, and a man. He tells me he does not know how to write any of those words, so I ask if I can teach him something. When he gives me permission, I say "Let's look at your sun. Sun starts like this -- SSSSSSun." Taking his hand, I reproduce an S with him, while we both say the word together. That's the only thing I want to teach him to write that day, because two things tend to get confused or lost. By the end of the year, Christopher is writing in sentences with punctuation, apostrophes, and some capital letters.

Next I go to Brian, who wants to know how to spell "apple." He can read on a second-grade level and thinks the word doesn't look right. Once I show him how to spell it, he takes the word and uses it.

Joshua looks stuck and says he doesn't know what to write about. I ask him to read what he wrote yesterday, and then I ask him some specific questions about what he wrote. I let him decide whether to use this dialogue as the basis for today's writing.

Amy is preparing to publish a book, so she's busy deciding what the title will be, who it will be dedicated to, where she wants the text, what kind of print she wants (traditional or primary), and if there will be any pictures. This information is filled in on a publishing form, which will also include biographical information about the author.

Publishing is a very important part of the writing process, and most children publish at least three or four books a year. By taking their writing and turning it into a book with a title, cover, dedication, and information about the author, publishing confirms children's ownership of the skills they have acquired in a most tangible way, and it allows them to share their accomplishments with others.

After five children have published books, we invite their parents to an Authors' Tea, where the children can read from their books and talk about them with the rest of the class, as well as any parents or friends who choose to attend. I ask the parents to bring a healthy snack for everyone, which we can enjoy along with juice, and I bring in a flower arrangement and butcher paper to cover the tables.

The children make a program for the event, and we have an announcer who introduces each author. The authors read their own stories and show their pictures, and, of course, the audience applauds. The authors then ask for comments from the audience, and afterwards they serve their guests a snack. It's a truly exciting celebration for the children, their parents, and the teacher.

If publishing a book is not possible, the same thing can be done with poetry or charts or other literary forms. You could have a poetry tea or a readers' tea, or some similar event. The main thing is to celebrate what the children can do, because it enriches the value of the experience for them.

One other important aspect of the writing process is record keeping. Each time a child masters something new, I write about it in the folder that's kept in their writing tray. This lets the children see how they are growing and encourages them to take more risks.

Another form of record keeping is to provide journals for each child, and let the child choose a favorite piece of writing to put in the journal each month. If monthly samples are too much, I would recommend saving the first writing of the year, a sample from around parent conference time in October, another sample from March, and a piece of writing from the end of the year. This helps the student, parent and teacher remember how much growth has occurred.

Lunch

My students and I have been fortunate to have lunch together everyday in our classroom. Now you might think "Fortunate? I wouldn't like that..." which is about what I thought when I was told that would be the procedure. But, I soon grew to love it, because it gave the children and me time to know each in a more personal way. We could sit and chat with each other, or...just be. Before long, the children were inviting family members or friends from other classes to join us for lunch, so it became very special.

Many of my charts grew out of this informal time, when the children's natural expressiveness was free to flow. For example, one day at lunch, Christopher was reciting a wonderful chant about dinosaurs, so I went over and asked him if he would teach it to me.

The next day, Christopher taught the chant to the entire class with the help of a chart, and in response the children made comments like "Christopher, I like that," and "Christopher, you did a good job." They also complimented him on his reading, and Christopher, who was an emergent reader, was beaming. His confidence in his reading ability increased, and believing he was a good reader helped make him a good reader. (Never underestimate the importance of a positive attitude!)

Christopher's brother came in from first grade at the end of the day and read Christopher's name on the chart. Christopher told him "Oh, I taught that to the children today," with a big smile on his face.

That's the sort of experience having lunch with your children can lead to.

Reading Process

The easiest way to start a reading process session is with a warm-up activity. Preparing for the warm-up is easy and inexpensive, because all that's needed is a large piece of paper with the words of a song or poem or rhyme or chant printed on it. This allows everyone to share the excitement of reading or singing or chanting together, and once the children have had a chance to participate in the process, they usually find it easier to listen and to learn. If you are just getting started with the Whole Language approach, this is a good way to begin.

After the warm-up, I read them a story they are already familiar with. We call this the old story, and while I let the children choose which story they want to hear, I ask them to choose one they have heard before. Our reading an old story together is reassuring for the children and helps them feel they can read it, too. It also makes them more secure about their ability to absorb the new story which comes next.

The new story is often part of an integrated theme, as themes are a particularly effective way of providing a meaningful context. The theme can be any topic you or the children might choose, ranging from a particular holiday to a particular author to a more general subject like science, poetry or music. Work on a particular theme might last for a day, a week, or more, and involve elements of other subjects such as math, history and art. Rather than focusing on these subjects individually, or on just reading and writing, you can incorporate them all into a theme and then teach through the theme.

This approach is particularly helpful for students who might be more interested in or more confident about subjects other than reading. But, it also helps all the students experience the full range of possibilities that reading provides. And, it lets them acquire and utilize skills in an interesting and enjoyable way.

For example, one week the theme might be Rick Charette's song, "Where Do My Sneakers Go At Night?" On Monday, we might just sing the song and brainstorm about ways to make sneakers part of our learning process. The next day, we share the song again, and I might ask the students to create a story about where their sneakers go. I would cut out paper to look like sneakers (with places for laces included), and the students could write their stories on "sneaker paper." Children love uniquely shaped books, paper, and text!

I might also ask them to bring in their sneakers the following day, so that after we read the story we could use them as part of a "whole math" lesson -- counting them; measuring them; comparing them; categorizing them by color, size, features, or even brand name; and then making a graph of the results. On Thursday, we might do sneaker art projects after sharing the song. Each student could have another sheet of sneaker paper on which to create his or her ideal sneaker, using crayons, felt-tip markers, and glitter or other add-ons.

By Friday, we might be ready to create our own Sneaker Big Book after sharing the song again. Depending on how many students are in the class, I might put a verse or part of a verse from the song on each page, so that all the children would have a page of their own to illustrate. Or, groups of children could work together on different pages. After illustrating their pages, they could all come up to the front of the room and line up holding their pages in front of them, so they could see the relationship of each page to the whole. Then, rather than combining all the pages to make an actual book, we might want to put them up on the wall side by side and let everyone "read the wall" when they want to.

With themes like these, you should also be ready to drop the idea and move on to something else if the children are bored. Their energy level, enjoyment, and commitment to the projects are important signals that should not be ignored. The same holds true when a project is so popular and exciting that the children don't want to stop. A theme expected to last a few days may go on for weeks, continuing to provide new learning opportunities every day.

For example, a second week of the sneaker theme could include a brainstorming session on Monday, in which children consider sneakers in relation to other types of footwear. Tuesday might be a day to organize a survey of what other students or parents wear on their feet, with the results compiled and graphed on Wednesday. On Thursday, I might provide partial drawings of different types of footwear and ask the children to complete them. And on Friday, the children might go

Building a theme "web".

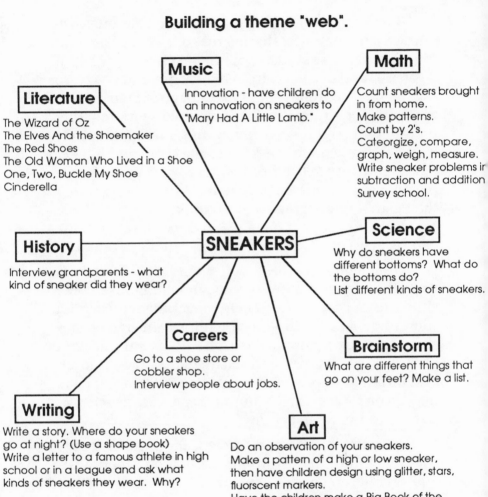

Music
Innovation - have children do an innovation on sneakers to "Mary Had A Little Lamb."

Math
Count sneakers brought in from home.
Make patterns.
Count by 2's.
Cateorgize, compare, graph, weigh, measure.
Write sneaker problems in subtraction and addition
Survey school.

Literature
The Wizard of Oz
The Elves And the Shoemaker
The Red Shoes
The Old Woman Who Lived in a Shoe
One, Two, Buckle My Shoe
Cinderella

SNEAKERS

Science
Why do sneakers have different bottoms? What do the bottoms do?
List different kinds of sneakers.

History
Interview grandparents - what kind of sneaker did they wear?

Careers
Go to a shoe store or cobbler shop.
Interview people about jobs.

Brainstorm
What are different things that go on your feet? Make a list.

Writing
Write a story. Where do your sneakers go at night? (Use a shape book)
Write a letter to a famous athlete in high school or in a league and ask what kinds of sneakers they wear. Why?

Art
Do an observation of your sneakers.
Make a pattern of a high or low sneaker, then have children design using glitter, stars, fluorscent markers.
Have the children make a Big Book of the song "Where Do My Sneakers Go At Night."
Use glitter, stars and dark blue paper.
Make pictures of what do you wear on feet.

P.S. Your ideas are probably better!

to another classroom to act out the sneaker song or share their Sneaker Big Book.

Themes also provide a great context for some work on phonics. Once the children become familiar with a song I've written out on a chart, I might point to a particular word written on the chart, say the word, and have everyone repeat it, so they can make the connection between the way the word looks and the way it sounds. Then I might put the pointer down and ask them to find the word again. Or, I might have them say the word slowly with me and ask them to match the sounds they hear in it with individual letters.

The teaching of phonics can be part of the Whole Language process right from the beginning of the school year, as long as it occurs within a meaningful context. (It should also be based on songs or stories or chants the children already know, because the brain first looks for something that is already familiar and then can link it to something new.) The teaching of skills -- capitalization, punctuation, etc. -- can be integrated in a similar way. This allows the children to learn skills and phonics as part of the communication process, rather than as abstract, isolated bits of information.

Almost anything can be an effective Whole Language theme or teaching material, if you utilize your creativity and that of your students. And, all sorts of things can be taught within the context of a theme.

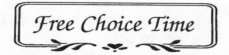

Free Choice Time

This is the time when children can choose any activity they want, so they may not work directly or even indirectly on reading and writing. However, this time can be an especially valuable Whole Language experience, because the children are free to pursue their own interests, and because the decisions they make provide me with information about how I can help them learn.

Supplies for this time period should be as diverse as possible and need not be expensive at all. The basics might include blocks, toy animals (including dinosaurs), a doll house with people, Legos, flannel boards, magnets, puppets, woodworking tools, clay, water colors, markers, colored paper, glue and paste. If available, water tables, sand tables, Cuisenaire rods, pattern blocks, teddy bear counters, and *Mathematics Their Way* supplies are a great help. But, most of all, I believe in using everyday materials such as scraps of cloth and wood, bottle caps, popsicle sticks, cardboard tubes from paper towel and toilet paper rolls, hangers, straws and anything else which prompts the children to use their imagination and creativity. (With 6 year-olds, I introduce these materials in an organized way in January.)

The use of everyday materials is particularly important because so many young children are being over-exposed to television, video games, store-bought products, and adult-directed play, which provide experiences that for the most part are mentally and physically passive. Children playing a video game might be making decisions and improving their hand-eye coordination, but they are doing so in a context that has been created for them. When they create their own toys and activities out of materials not designed for such purposes, then they are molding the world around them rather than being molded by it. Not only is this sort of activity good for them, it is also so popular that the children often have to take turns so that everyone gets a chance to participate.

In a similar way, free-choice time allows children to take an active, imaginative approach to their own education. For example, one day a student named Brian chooses to work by himself and observe a feather. Rather than play with it, he wants to study it, draw it, and write down his observations. His father is a scientist, and clearly Brian is becoming one, too. Writing helps him further his scientific interests, and his scientific interests lead to further writing.

A student named Robert sits down one day and writes a song. It's a silly song about not speaking Spanish, but Robert has a wonderful sense of humor and this experience lets him enjoy creating and writing. The fact that the song is about language also tells me that he is thinking about language and working on it in his own way.

Information like this, combined with my observations about how children interact and what decisions they make, is one of the great benefits of free choice time. Often I just sit down with my clipboard and make notes on what children are doing and how they relate socially. I can make use of this information later by providing a brief amount of direct instruction, or by integrating it into my activities throughout the school day.

At other times, I might use free choice time to talk with a child who feels bad because "Daddy left...and he's not coming back...and Mom's sad." Or, I might use some of the time to help a child finish publishing a book.

Whether I'm observing or actively involved, free choice time lets the children and I end the school day with an opportunity to think for ourselves and make our own decisions. After all, that is what a good education should lead to, isn't it?

Whole Language Evaluations

You will be required to take a test when you finish reading this chapter. Without referring to the book, you'll have to provide written answers to questions kept secret from you until then. You'll be expected to summarize all the concepts presented in this chapter, and you'll be penalized for any grammatical or spelling errors. Your answers will be compared with those of other people you know who are also reading this book, and the way they answer the questions will affect your grade. Everyone will know how well or how poorly you do, and if you make too many mistakes, you will have to read the chapter again while everyone else goes outside to play.

Doesn't make you too enthusiastic about reading the chapter, does it?

In fact, if you or I did have to read the chapter under such circumstances, we would probably be more than a little distracted. We might want to stop from time to time in order to focus on the key concepts and memorize them. We might start trying to anticipate what the questions will be, and we might find it difficult to concentrate simply because we're feeling anxious about the test and have difficulty coping with our discomfort.

Imagine how much more difficult this would be for young children who are still uncertain about their ability to read and write. Their relationships with their peers and their self-esteem are also less secure, while things we take for granted -- such as the ability to grasp a pencil correctly, comprehend abstract concepts, and sit still for extended periods of time -- may be sources of great difficulty for them.

Now here's a surprise quiz: Does the way we evaluate students affect their ability to learn? ( ) Yes ( ) No

If you answered yes, you can keep reading. If you answered no, you just flunked the quiz, and I want you to write "I must pay more attention to my students" 25 times on the nearest chalkboard before reading any further.

Those of you who answered yes probably know that the effects of testing extend beyond the students themselves. Many teachers (and their supervisors) are also evaluated on the basis of students' test scores. So, there is pressure on teachers to "teach to the test" by presenting test-related material in formats that resemble the tests. As a result, more than a few primary school classrooms resemble cram courses in which the curriculum and teaching methods are determined by test makers rather than teachers, administrators, or local school boards.

As a Whole Language teacher, I believe the curriculum should be responsive to students' interests and build on their strengths. I also believe that accurate evaluations should be an integral part of this process, providing important information about students' progress by documenting what has been accomplished in the classroom. Whole Language evaluations should therefore be derived from the curriculum, as opposed to deriving the curriculum from the evaluations.

Another guiding principle for Whole Language evaluations has to do with the way students are treated in the classroom. In a Whole Language classroom where cooperation is emphasized, children learn from each other and help each other grow. In more traditional classrooms where competitive grading systems are used, students strive to do better than their peers, which often leads to feelings of anger, jealousy, fear, and sadness. A few children may feel like winners in such an environment, but many feel like losers.

Especially when children are learning to read and write, they need to be supported rather than discouraged, to be reminded about what they have accomplished rather than made to feel inferior. Children may be ready to compete academically in later years, but forcing them to compete when they are just beginning to define themselves and acquire basic skills is counterproductive and unfair.

Instead of comparing students with each other, a Whole Language teacher can evaluate students by comparing them with themselves -- showing them the progress they have made over time. This approach provides reinforcement for accomplishments and clearly identifies those areas in need of improvement, without pitting each student against the rest of the class. It also emphasizes students' actual accomplishments in the classroom, rather than dubious comparisons to "norms" based on different students from different areas who are taught different material in different ways. Most of all, it can make evaluations of reading and writing ability a source of pride and enjoyment, rather than a source of anxiety or negativity.

The following sections of this chapter explain a range of techniques for evaluating students and effectively utilizing evaluation results.

Writing

In a Whole Language classroom, the main way children learn to write is by writing, so it naturally follows that the main way of evaluating their progress is to look at the changes in their writing that occur during the school year. This can be done most effectively and easily by collecting samples from students' journals on a regular basis, as often as once a month or more, and keeping them in a portfolio. Students can participate in selecting their best examples as part of this process, which helps them learn to evaluate and value their own writing.

By the end of the school year, the progress that has been made will be evident. And, just as important, areas where additional help is needed can also be identified. Phonics, punctuation, grammar, content, sequence, handwriting -- all can be evaluated as they naturally occur, rather than based on contrived test questions administered in a contrived situation.

The portfolio can be shared with administrators and other teachers who want to learn more about individual students or the class as a whole. It also makes a great tool for parent-teacher conferences, because the teacher can show the parent what the child is actually doing. And, it's a wonderful experience to review a portfolio with the student who created it, because children often forget where they started and how much progress they made. In this way, evaluation can lead to feelings of pride and accomplishment, as well as a better understanding of the growth process.

In addition to the samples themselves, I also make use of the folder. At the top of one side of the folder the words "Things I Know" are printed, and during the year I write down accomplishments and share them with the children. Starting a sentence with capital letters, using exclamation points, learning new words -- any significant signs of progress can be noted and used as an occasion to provide immediate positive reinforcement, as well as a reminder for the future.

Two other evaluations I have found particularly helpful were devised by Marie Clay and are described in her book, *The Early Detection of Reading Difficulties*. One is a ten-minute writing vocabulary test in which the children are asked to write all the words they know. The children receive one point for each word that is spelled correctly. During the test, I like to provide prompts by asking questions such as "Can you write your name? Do you know the words 'Mom' and 'Dad'?" Marie Clay offers numerous suggestions for implementing the evaluation and interpreting the results, which provide information about writing and spelling as well as vocabulary.

The other evaluation of hers I particularly like is a dictation test, in which the teacher reads a sentence and the children write down what they hear. This provides a lot of information in regard to children's use of inventive and formal spelling, punctuation, capitals, etc.

I give both the vocabulary test and the dictation test two or three times during the year, so the children and I have a record of their progress similar to that provided by the portfolios and journals. The results help me learn about my students and help the students learn about themselves. The children are more comfortable with these sorts of evaluations because the evaluations are meaningful, open-ended, and emphasize what the children can do.

Reading

Evaluations of children's reading utilize similar concepts. Portfolios combined with a limited number of tests support the children's development and provide needed information, without having a negative impact on the curriculum.

A reading portfolio is comprised of two key elements: tape recordings of the children actually reading material they selected, and written lists of books the children chose to read.

To create tape-recorded reading portfolios, I provide each child with his or her own tape at the beginning of the year. On a regular basis -- perhaps once every two months -- the children read material of their choosing into the tape recorder's microphone. With the tape stopped, I then ask a few comprehension questions regarding the plot, characters, predictions, etc. As this process continues during the year, the children's progress and patterns of development are captured on tape. And, the children can listen to tapes of themselves reading, which they love. I also ask their permission to make some comments on the tape, and if they agree, I give them some positive feedback which they can also replay.

In addition, children can be asked to summarize rather than read stories, in order to capture information about their comprehension and sense of sequence. More detailed interviews about stories can also be tape recorded, providing a record of children's reading and verbal ability.

Like portfolios of writing, tape recordings of children reading are wonderful to share during parent conferences, because they present information about the child in a readily understandable form. I also suggest that parents provide some positive feedback on the tape, so the children can listen to that as well as their own reading.

Lists of books that children have read aloud to the teacher also provide important information, especially when the children choose the books. Special interests, levels of ability, and other indications of a child's individual learning process can be gleaned, especially if the list includes the date, the pages read, and any comments. Children who have reached first grade or beyond can do their own record-keeping, which helps them use their skills in a meaningful way as well as participate in the evaluation process.

Marie Clay's "Concepts About Print," which is also from *The Early Detection of Reading Difficulties*, is a one-on-one test usually given by district reading consultants at the beginning of the kindergarten and first grade years, and again at the end of each year. Children are given a book and asked to show where the front of the book is, where the print starts, what direction it goes in, and other questions about the student's level of understanding.

Another effective evaluation devised by Marie Clay, which can also be found in *The Early Detection of Reading Difficulties*, is her "Diagnostic Survey." It and Ken Goodman's "Miscue Analysis," which can be found in *The Whole Language Evaluation Book*, explain how to take a "running record" of the child's reading ability. This identifies both strengths and weaknesses, but emphasizes building on strengths.

Putting It All Together

The evaluations described above can be used to determine whether a student receives the usual A, B, C, D, or F. Portfolios -- including both writing samples and tape recordings -- can be combined with checklists, student projects, anecdotal records, and even traditional quizzes and tests, then boiled down to a single mark. However, in many cases this approach is inaccurate, unfair, and does lasting damage.

Using standard letter or numeral marks in the early primary grades can warp the learning process much like standardized testing does. The diversity of children's capabilities, their struggles to overcome disadvantages, their enthusiasm and love of learning cannot adequately be summed up by a single letter or number. And, too often, such grades become self-fulfilling prophecies for young children who are just beginning to define themselves and still believe that teacher knows best.

Letter and numeral grades are also far better suited to a phonics-oriented approach which emphasizes isolated skills rather than meaningful wholes, correctness rather than communication, and distinct subjects rather than integrated themes. A grading system well suited to the Whole Language approach must give greater recognition to the diversity and richness of the learning process.

Report cards that give equal weight to a range of intellectual, social, and emotional factors provide a far more balanced and informative means of evaluating a young child's achievements and progress. Traditionally, the social and emotional aspects of a child's development, if they are covered at all, tend to be found down in one corner and viewed as unimportant, while the 3 R's take center stage. Yet, for young children in particular, the forming of positive attitudes -- toward learning, other people and oneself -- is far more important than the particular grade received. Additional skills can always be acquired later if a student has a positive attitude, but the best education in the world will be wasted on a student who is resistant to learning.

Different grades for performance and effort are also important, because some children perform well with little effort, while others try very hard but still do not perform well.

Unfortunately, many teachers are simply not allowed to alter their school's report cards. They may be able to create additional report cards of their own, however, which can be used as supplements, if not replacements.

The key to creating a curriculum-based grading system is to identify the goals you want students to accomplish. This can include broad objectives such as writing independently, communicating thoughts and feelings clearly, and using sentences. Students can be graded according to these standards in ways that provide helpful information, which can then be reviewed with parents as well as other educators.

Providing helpful information about students does little good if it is not put to use. Reviewing evaluations with parents is therefore a vital part of the process. If parents can discuss areas needing improvement and ways to assist their child, they are more likely to help and the child is more likely to do well in school.

Evaluation reviews create opportunities to explain the importance of reading to children every night and discussing stories with them. The value of working at home with crayons, paint, clay, pencils, scissors and Legos should also be explained to the parents of children who are learning to write. And, parents can learn to encourage their children to write at home through activities such as writing notes to each other, making shopping lists together, and helping the child create a personal photograph album or telephone book. These sorts of suggestions complete the evaluation process by making use of the information which has been gathered about the child.

Teachers are obviously the people best equipped to evaluate their students, and they need to take part in creating evaluations, as well as communicating the results to others. Teachers at each grade level can meet with their counterparts in the grades above and below theirs to provide continuity and a sense of shared purpose -- deciding what children should know, how they should learn, and how the learning process should be measured.

The revision of evaluations and report cards should be an ongoing process, just like learning and teaching are. When teachers participate in the process, they can integrate evaluation with the other events taking place in the classroom, so that it, too, is a meaningful and appropriate part of the Whole Language experience.

Dear Carol,
Believe in who
you are ⭐

The
Whole Language
Teacher

You already are
a shining star ⭐
So... just keep
shining! Love to you!

57

When students gave me samples of their writing to put in their portfolios, I used to put the date on the front page with a rubber stamp. One day I noticed that the children grew angry when I did this, because I was putting marks on their papers and they wanted to use the stamp just like a "grownup." They had a sense of ownership about what they had written, and they wanted to complete their work themselves. So, I showed them how to use the stamp and let them put the date on their own papers, which they quickly began to enjoy doing.

As a Whole Language teacher, my most important responsibility is to pay attention to my students. Whether they tell me things directly or just provide clues which I can observe and interpret, they are giving me the information I need to be an effective teacher. Once I understand a child, I can build on his or her strengths, so as to increase self-esteem and develop a positive attitude about learning. I can also help the children work through their weak areas by creating an environment where they feel safe taking risks and making mistakes. Accepting children as they are is the prerequisite for teaching Whole Language effectively.

A vital part of this process is giving children the opportunity to make choices. I used to tell students what to do and where to do it. Now, as much as possible, I let the children choose what they want to read and write, and I let them sit wherever they want. (They end up sitting in the same place every day.) I call this "freedom within structure."

Children taught in this way are active participants in the learning process, rather than passive recipients of information and skill training. And, one of the primary benefits of this approach is that students' spans of attention tend to be much longer, because the work is joyful and meaningful for them. Children's attention spans usually shrink when they are forced to do something they don't want to do, as their focus remains split between what they want to do and what they are supposed to do.

If I notice that my students' attention spans seem to be growing short, I try to observe them more closely and determine the cause. Usually, there's something I can do to shift gears and help them stay involved in a learning experience. When I respond to the children, instead of requiring them to respond to me, everyone wins.

Of course, there is much more to being a Whole Language teacher than simply paying attention to children and giving them freedom. The following overview covers several other important aspects of the teaching process.

Classroom Preparation

A well-organized but comfortable classroom makes a big difference in children's behavior. If the teacher creates an environment that lets students feel relaxed yet encourages them to learn, behavior problems are much less likely to occur.

Children know immediately if the classroom is their room or the teacher's room. If the learning materials are easily accessible to them, and if they can use everything they see, they will experience much less frustration and be less dependent on the teacher. If, on the other hand, the classroom is organized for the teacher's convenience, or with an emphasis on exerting control over the students, the stage has been set for student-teacher conflicts. The children will feel uncomfortable and express their discomfort by acting out in various ways -- distracting themselves and the teacher from the learning process.

Creating a "homey" environment also helps in this regard. A classroom which contains rocking chairs, pillows, rugs, plants, and a playhouse with curtains on its windows makes school an extension of home, rather than an alien world. Children in such an environment find it easier to concentrate and to enjoy the learning process precisely because they feel comfortable and supported.

One teacher recently told me her daughter did not like to read in school because it wasn't comfortable. If that sounds like a childish excuse, it may be worth remembering that many adults have a favorite "easy chair" just for reading (is that where you're reading this book?), and children who are learning to read and write deserve all the help they can get.

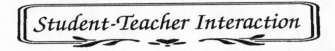

Student-Teacher Interaction

The ways in which a Whole Language teacher relates to students also have a profound effect on behavior and learning process. Children experience their teachers as individual people as well as educators, and often the personal interaction between child and adult is just as important as the formal relationship between student and teacher.

Most of us can remember favorite teachers who made school interesting and even fun. Such teachers may have been early role models, and they may have helped us make important discoveries about ourselves or attain unexpected goals. They may even have become lifelong friends. While their ability as teachers had much to do with the impact they made, often it was the way they conducted themselves as individuals that made them such important people in our lives.

When talking with a group of teachers, I often stand on a chair in the midst of the audience, so they can see how big they look to children. I consider this one of the most important aspects of teaching -- remembering that you are a big, powerful yet distanced figure in their lives, and they literally look up to you. Often, the facial features that stand out from this perspective are the nostrils and the chin, which can make someone look angry or even mean.

To counteract this image, I often work "below" the students and give them the power! Coming down to their level, by using a small chair or crouching, makes it easier for us to work together. And, it helps to create an environment in which the children and I can relate to each other as individuals, not just student and teacher or child and adult.

As a Whole Language teacher, I believe one of the most important things I can do is to be "real," to share who I am and what I do with my life. I try to let my students know what I was like when I was young, and what life is like for me now. This helps them understand me, and it can help them understand themselves, so that they feel more comfortable about school and their learning process.

When I was new to teaching, I thought I had to greet my students with a smile every day, even if I really felt angry or sad inside. But I soon found that children would immediately begin to act out on days when I felt badly, because I was giving them a double message. They could sense how I really felt and that I wasn't being honest with them. They thought it was their fault, and since I was creating an environment in which feelings could not be honestly expressed, they showed their discomfort by acting out in other ways.

Now, when I'm having a bad day, I say so right away and explain why. This lets the children know that it's not their fault and helps them understand that teachers have good days and bad days, just like they do. It also makes it easier for them to tell me about things that affect their behavior and learning ability, which in turn helps me to be a more responsive and effective teacher.

Similarly, if I do things I said I wouldn't do, or if I don't do things that I've promised to do, I apologize and ask forgiveness and explain what happened. This helps to create an environment in which children feel safe to make the mistakes needed for growth, and it shows children how they can handle mistakes they make.

Another important teaching practice is fairness. If a teacher favors one child in particular, the others will know who the "class pet" is. And the others will feel the teacher is telling them that they're not good enough. So, they'll act out and not try their best, because the teacher has set them up to lose no matter what they do.

The same principle applies to the teacher's personal relationship with each student. Do you think children can sense whether you like them or not? Of course they can, even though they may not be able to articulate it or understand why. And, don't you think that affects the way they perform in the classroom?

In every moment of every day, we either lift children up, or we put them down. If children think you don't like them, they're likely to respond by doing just enough to get by, and acting out. But, if they sense that you like or love them, they'll believe in themselves and work twice as hard. One of the wonderful things about Whole Language is that it helps teachers and students build positive relationships, instead of getting caught in the old-fashioned roles of disciplinarians and trouble-makers.

Another aspect of fairness has to do with competition among students. Even when competition is overt and all the rules are followed, it can be very detrimental to young children. Some children may win, but too many others lose. I believe every child wants to learn every day and every child wants to win every day, so that's what I try to have happen in my classroom every day. Children benefit far more when they compete with themselves -- do better than they've done in the past --

than when they compete with each other.

In sum, a primary rule for Whole Language teachers is the golden rule -- treating students the way we would want to be treated. We all prefer to have our thoughts and feelings respected, so that's how we should treat the children in our care.

Teaching By Demonstration

Just as children observe and respond to a teacher's personal attributes, they are also shaped by the way in which a teacher carries out professional responsibilities. Whole Language provides an activity-oriented approach to learning, with much reading and writing taking place in the classroom, and it requires an activity-oriented approach to teaching, as well.

A teacher who encourages students to read and write, but does little reading and writing herself in the classroom, is sending a double message. The old expression "Do as I say, not as I do" is not appropriate for a Whole Language classroom. A Whole Language teacher must read and write in the classroom every day, because children who frequently observe adults reading and writing -- both at school and at home -- recognize that these are valuable activities worth pursuing.

In addition to communicating directly with students through reading and writing, teachers can also model reading and writing on a daily basis through record keeping. From taking attendance to making notes about student activities to evaluating students' reading and writing, a Whole Language teacher can show students that the skills they are learning are an important part of her job.

In a traditional classroom, some of these tasks are often done hurriedly, or when children are out of the classroom, or even after school. In a Whole Language classroom, with its emphasis on process, record keeping is easier to include in the daily routine because the children spend more time working on their own or with each other, freeing the teacher to observe and record rather than constantly lecturing and trying to keep students quiet. And, as children become more proficient at reading and writing, they can participate and assist in the maintenance of some records, which further reinforces the value of the activity.

Sharing written records with children is especially important in this regard. Records of books they have read and books they have written can be kept with their reading and writing materials, so the children can refer to them and understand the benefits of keeping them. In the same way, an open record of group activities can provide an educational response to a complaint such as "Mary always gets to go first."

Along with specific skills such as reading and writing, a Whole Language teacher also demonstrates a commitment to learning and growth. One of the advantages of the Whole Language approach is that its emphasis on observation and responsiveness encourages teachers to keep learning about children's interests and growth processes. And the emphasis on child-initiated activities generates new opportunities and challenges, rather than forcing teachers to keep repeating the same skill drills year after year. A teacher who welcomes new insights and new ways to learn is setting a very important example for young students.

One day my students went out on a field trip with an environmentalist from a conservation center, and when they came back they wanted to make a big book about animals and their tracks. I had never thought about doing such a project, but I followed their lead and innovated. We created a book in which the right-hand page showed the tracks of an animal with some text like "Look, I see some tracks!", and the following page contained an illustration of the animal, along with its name and information about it. From little animals such as squirrels, skunks, beavers and raccoons, the book went on to big animals like deer and bears, ending with people tracks. This project let the children learn about science, art, writing and reading, while I learned about their interests and abilities, and about animal tracks.

If you demonstrate creativity and initiative, your students are likely to do the same. Whole Language helps in this regard, because it's not something a teacher can buy. All the curriculum materials do not come in one convenient package, and there's no curriculum guide that will tell you what to say and do every day. You can buy some of the materials you use, and you can get some of your ideas from other sources, but the success of the Whole Language approach depends on what happens between you and your students. If you love teaching, and you share your talent, your knowledge, and the things that you love, your students will love learning and learn well.

Teachers may also have skills they would like to improve, and doing so in the classroom can be helpful for children. For example, if I have doubts about my ability as an artist, I may tell my students that and work with them when they're practicing drawing. We may all try to draw a flower, and during the process I can help them and myself by asking questions such as "Do you notice anything about the leaves on the stem?", "What about the petals on the flower?", "What's inside the flower?" and "What colors do you see?" Meanwhile, I'm drawing my own picture, and the children's observations and encouragement can help me just as my comments help them. Most importantly, they have the satisfaction of knowing that they can make important contributions to others' growth, and that even teachers need to practice and improve.

Professional Growth

Learning is a process of growth for children, and teaching Whole Language is also a growth process -- a process of revising and changing and becoming. Most

Whole Language teachers find the process so fulfilling that their involvement in the process keeps increasing, so they continue to go to conferences and workshops, and to share information and ideas with other professionals informally.

One way this can happen on a local level is through TAWL (Teachers Applying Whole Language) groups. These groups can now be found in many parts of the U.S., where they meet a few times each year. They provide a forum in which teachers can share ideas and techniques, as well as support the growth process in other ways. There is often a big gap between beginning Whole Language teachers and those who have several years of experience, and informal discussions outside the school can be an effective way to bridge the gap. Some TAWL groups also give awards to administrators, school boards, and other members of the education community who have helped to implement the Whole Language approach.

Attending Whole Language workshops can also be an effective means of professional growth. Good workshops not only let teachers learn from experts, they provide opportunities for teachers to meet and share ideas with each other. A good Whole Language workshop should resemble a Whole Language classroom, in that interaction and responsiveness are encouraged.

In-service days, when consultants work directly with teachers in the schools, can have a major impact on the development of Whole Language classes if properly done. I was recently told that Canadian teachers have up to 20 in-service days in their districts each year, which clearly represents a sustained commitment to professional growth. In the U.S., unfortunately, there is a tendency to bring in a consultant for a day or two and then never follow-up. This is obviously a much less effective approach, because teachers need support and feedback over time, not just in small, isolated doses.

Obtaining the funding for workshops and sustained in-service can, of course, be a problem, and that leads to what I consider another important aspect of a Whole Language teacher's professional growth -- being political. By political, I do not necessarily mean participating in marches or going door-to-door in a community, although such activities can be part of the process. Instead, I mean an active involvement in explaining to the community what its children need. Talking to parents at the school, or even in the grocery store, can be political action. So can having parents and administrators visit your classroom, where they often end up expressing awe at how hard a teacher works and how much is accomplished despite all the difficulties.

When the door to the classroom is open to outsiders, and they can see the sparkle in the children's eyes as well as all the problems, then support for the teacher grows. Parents and administrators who want more individual attention for the children will support funding for smaller classes. Parents and administrators who want better trained teachers will support funding for more workshops and in-service days.

Working well with others is the key to success, whether the others are students, parents, or educators. Sometimes, belief in a philosophy like Whole Language can lead to zealotry, with others being attacked or put down for holding opposing or even slightly different points of view. I find that sharing, supporting, and modeling are far more effective means of accomplishing goals, outside the classroom as well as inside.

Making Parents Part Of The Whole Language Process

Recently I went to an American Indian dance festival and saw a little two-year-old child doing a beautiful dance. Someone in the audience asked the parents how they taught their child to dance so beautifully, and one of the parents replied "We don't teach the children. We watch the children and see what they do, and that becomes their dance."

Just as a Whole Language teacher carefully observes students in the classroom and supports their interests as part of the learning process, parents can use a similar approach at home to help their children learn to read and write. And, through their understanding and support of Whole Language process, parents can also make important contributions to classroom activities, helping their children and the teacher.

As a beginning teacher I was afraid of parents, but over the years I found that parents can be my most valuable asset. In fact, parents are almost as important to the Whole Language process as the children themselves, so communicating effectively with parents is vital.

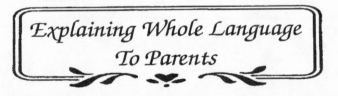

Explaining Whole Language To Parents

Like children, parents often have difficulty understanding things they have never experienced, so Whole Language is best explained to them in terms of what they have experienced.

By this, I don't mean how they learned to read and write. That experience probably consisted of a basal reader and a workbook, with new spelling words on Monday, a review on Thursday, and the spelling test on Friday. It was a matter of writing what the teacher told them to write, and doing it correctly as soon as possible. As this approach is far removed from Whole Language, I've found that two other types of experiences offer parents much better insights into the value of the Whole Language process.

The first approach is to ask parents how they taught their children to talk, and as different answers are volunteered, write down the essentials of each on a chalk board or an overhead.

Some parents might say they taught their children by talking to them, and if you ask what they talked about, they'll probably say they talked about things that were part of the children's environment. The parents pointed to things and named them, often having the children touch them as well. And the parents probably talked about activities, family members and other aspects of the life the child directly experienced through the five senses, so it was all "meaningful" to the child.

Another answer might be that parents read to the child, and usually they read stories the children enjoyed, like nursery rhymes. If the child didn't like the story, he or she might push the book away, cry, or resist in some other way. So the child helped choose the story or book the parent read, and the reading material was based on the child's interests.

One parent might add that taking children on trips helped them learn to talk, because they saw new things and learned new names for them. Again, this sort of learning grew out of the children's direct experience of the world around them.

Singing is another way some children learned to use words. Even parents who don't think they sing well have found that something important happens when they sing to children. The children just stop and look and listen and love it. (As a teacher, anything you sing will naturally be learned by the child! I promise!) Anything else the parents did with children? Well, hopefully they played with the children, and they let the children pretend to be different people or animals or objects. This helped children learn to use new words and sounds through "make-believe" experiences.

Some parents might also admit they encouraged their children by accepting approximations of words. Let's say, for example, that the child already knows how to say "Daddy." Of course, Mom wants the child to say "Mom" right away, but that's a little harder to pronounce. So, Mom might sit holding the child saying "Momma loves you", and if the child says "Mmmmuh, mmmmuh," then Mom hugs the child and says "Oh, you said Momma. That's wonderful." And, the child looks at Mom and thinks "Oh, I did something wonderful." The next thing you know, the child is saying "Momma, cookie," and before long it will be "Mom, can I have the keys to the car?", at which point old Mom is saying "No way."

One other thing parents often did, although they may not think of this as a means of education, is that they cherished their children just for being. Love is a basic human need, and this emotional bonding led the child to model activities that the parent demonstrated, so that many learning experiences occurred naturally without formal attempts at education. It also let the children feel safe enough to take the risks needed to learn through trial and error.

Now, let's summarize this list we've created. Parents taught their children to talk by:

Naming objects children could see and touch
Reading stories children liked
Taking trips which provided new experiences
Singing to children
Letting children play
Encouraging approximations of words
Cherishing children

The end result was that the children picked up the language in a natural, sequential way -- being surrounded with meaningful language, feeling very safe at first, then taking risks and approximating. As they continued approximating and trying new words, they began to develop a rich vocabulary.

At this point, you might ask the parents if they think children can learn to read the same way they learned to talk. You know many of them will answer "Yes."

If we taught children to talk the same way we teach them to read and write, a lot of them might never say "Mom." The organized, linear, structured approach makes sense to minds that think that way, but that's not how young children think and learn.

The natural process of teaching children to read and write requires us to tell children what they are doing right every day, to surround them with print that has meaning to them, to provide them with experiences that have meaning for them, and then let them write about it all. This is a very positive process, and that's important because children grow by taking risks, and they will only take risks when they feel safe. One of our most important responsibilities as teachers and parents is to create a safe environment in which children are willing to take the risks needed to grow.

A second way to introduce parents to Whole Language is to ask whether any have travelled to a foreign country where they didn't know the language. Then ask those who have had that experience how they learned the language while they were there.

Anyone who drove probably learned to read road signs, and those who took public transportation learned words like "ticket" and "time". Most people learned to identify certain foods and certain numbers, as well as the local currency. And just about everyone learned a few key phrases like "Where is the bathroom?"

Now ask how many bothered to memorize the alphabet after they arrived in the country. The answer will probably be none. I've been going to Mexico for 25 years, but I still can't recite the alphabet in Spanish.

So, all this learning of the language took place, but learning the alphabet was not part of the process. Instead, the adults learned in "wholes" -- either whole words or whole phrases -- and that's one way children learn, too. Young children are in a country where they don't know the language, but when they go to the grocery store they can identify their favorite cereal, their favorite candy bar, and their favorite ice cream. They also know all their friends' names, because these are words that are important to them.

Whole Language lets children learn from their interests and needs, just like grown-ups do. And, because the information they learn this way is meaningful to them, learning is easier and the children want to learn more.

Meeting With Parents

Like children, parents quickly sense whether you respect them and care about them. I find it helpful to have a series of get-togethers with parents during the year, and whenever parents come to the school, I make a point of saying their names, shaking hands with them, and welcoming them at the door.

Just before the school year begins, I invite the students and their entire families to an "open house" in the classroom. Parents, grandparents, brothers and sisters -- everyone is welcome. This approach helps people feel comfortable, and if the family feels comfortable in the classroom, the child will, too.

Having food available is also important, because food conveys a very special message. It says "I care about you. I like you. I expect you. I want to nurture you."

Another important aspect of the meeting is a sign-up sheet for parent volunteers. This should include a place for information about any special interests or activities parents might want to share with children. Some possibilities include cooking, helping to write and publish books, preparing costumes, driving during field trips, tape recording stories, making flannel boards stories, and collecting buttons, wood scraps, and other "good junk" that can be a helpful part of the learning process.

The sign-up sheet also lets parents know they are welcome in the classroom. And as a teacher, I know that when parents are in the classroom, they see what I am trying to do, they see their child learning, and they see their child in relation to all the other children. This makes parents much more likely to be supportive.

Rather than discuss Whole Language in detail at this meeting, I invite the parents to another meeting five days after school starts. To keep the number of absentee parents low, I ask the students to help. Parents are much more likely to attend when asked directly by their children. It also helps if the children have made name tags for their parents and left notes about their work on display in the classroom, whether Lego designs, pattern blocks, clay objects or writing folders.

At this second meeting, I already feel comfortable with the parents, and they feel comfortable with me. I try to enhance this feeling by arranging the chairs in a circle for this meeting, so we all have the feeling that we are equals working together. This makes it easier to introduce them to Whole Language, using the techniques described earlier in this chapter.

I also explain the daily schedule during this meeting, and I give everyone a copy of the schedule to take home. We also review samples of children's writing, and we read a Big Book together. Experiencing these things for themselves helps parents understand and support their children.

This is also a good time to explain how the teaching of phonics and skills is included in the Whole Language process. Parents who are concerned about the Whole Language approach often feel reassured when they understand that Whole Language does not exclude the teaching of phonics and skills -- it provides a context in which phonics and skills make sense to children and are therefore easier to learn.

Private conferences with parents usually follow the second meeting, first in November and then again in the spring. I have found a number of ways to make the conferences more relaxed and productive. After meeting parents at the door, sitting beside them creates a better atmosphere than sitting behind a desk, because the desk becomes a boundary between teacher and parent and creates an environment in which opposition is more likely to occur.

Starting with a general question like "How do you think school is going for your child?" usually provides a lot of information about the child and the parent. Surprisingly, many parents are never asked this question, even though it gives them an opportunity to open up and provide important information. Having some of the child's work on hand -- writing, artwork, or some other project -- provides a focal point for the discussion and an opportunity to show the parent how the child is progressing.

I also try to praise the parent for their contributions to the child's education. If the parent is reading to the child, I let them know there is a high correlation between parents reading to children and children wanting to read. I encourage parents to continue reading to and with their children right through high school and beyond. Reading together makes reading more fun and significant for children, and it creates a bond between parent and child. It also leads to family discussions, which are an important part of the child's learning process.

When there's a need to talk about something negative, I try to make it the only negative aspect I discuss. And I've learned not to blame the parent, because that just creates opposition instead of a working relationship. One approach I've found effective is to describe a problem I'm having in the classroom and ask if the parent has noticed anything similar at home. This gives the parent options, and whatever the response, I then describe how I try to work through the problem with the child. The parent can then go home and try the approach without ever having acknowledged their own difficulty dealing with the problem.

For example, I might say that I noticed Christopher has a hard time listening, and then I ask if this ever happens at home. If a parents answers "yes," we have a reason to share information and work together. If the answer is "no," I can still explain how I try to handle it and actually demonstrate what I do -- such as touching the child on the shoulder, asking him to look at me, and asking him to repeat what I just said, to make sure he understands.

As the parents leave, I remind them of the wonderful things their children do, and I suggest they share these details with the children, so the children will have a sense that they are doing well in school.

Evening events can also provide extremely important opportunities to share with parents, and the events don't have to be a lot of work. A sing-along around Christmas time can be very successful, with the words and music to Christmas carols having been written on charts and taught to the children. The room can be decorated with artwork and centerpieces made by the children, and it can be lit with candles. One child then uses a flashlight to illuminate the chart for each song. Parents can bring treats and sing along with their children, while also observing how their children relate to the charts.

Another possibility is a teddy bear evening. We read the book *Hairy Bear* to the parents as a group, then acted it out using puppets the class made. Some children also acted out a jump rope teddy bear song, and of course, we had to perform the "Three Bears" play. Teddy bear cookies that we made for ourselves were served to our guests. So, the whole experience showed parents how reading, drama, art, costumes and even math (used in cooking) were combined in a Whole Language learning experience.

It was a great celebration, which is important, too. When we celebrate what children can do, and share the celebration with a larger audience, it becomes even more important and meaningful.

To complete the school year for the parents who have helped in the classroom, the principal and teachers at my school organize a special "thank you" luncheon in May. The principal personally invites each parent, and the teachers volunteer to make sandwiches, drinks, and, of course, dessert. Others bring in linen table cloths, silver candle holders, and beautiful bouquets of flowers.

Parents, teachers, and administrators have an elegant lunch together, celebrating all the work that's been done throughout the year. Everyone has an opportunity to interact and express their thanks, making it a truly memorable event. A write-up is usually sent to the local newspaper, in order to provide further recognition for those involved.

Other Forms Of Communication

Communication with parents should not be limited to meetings. Consider telephoning parents just to tell them about something wonderful their child did. They'll be beaming from ear to ear for the rest of the day. Or, how about a postcard reporting something positive that happened in school? You know it will end up right on the refrigerator.

I ask my principal for three postcards to send to each child and/or parent. After addressing them in August, I can mail them easily throughout the year. Sending an occasional postcard to the principal, or even a school board member, can also be a good idea.

A newsletter can be a very effective way of communicating with parents. It lets them know what you're doing in school, so they can support their child, and it lets them know that you care about keeping them informed. It also provides opportunities to encourage parent involvement with the class.

Parental Assistance In The Classroom

Parent volunteers can provide all sorts of valuable help in the classroom. In addition to the types of activities mentioned earlier -- typing stories and creating books, cooking, helping with artwork, organizing a field trip -- a few may have special talents they can share, such as quilting or helping to stage a play. You can always find ways to make special projects part of the Whole Language process, by linking them to a reading or writing experience.

Another important benefit of having parent volunteers is that when they spend time in the classroom, they'll support you one hundred percent. One parent who came in only twenty minutes a week thought I should be wearing a halo and sprouting wings. She said "I've only been here twenty minutes and I'm totally worn out. How do you do this all day and all week?"

Not only do such parents support individual teachers, they also support the school budget because they recognize how hard teachers work.

And, don't forget that parents who help deserve to be thanked. My students and I might sing to them from our charts, or use the old chant "Two, four, six, eight, who do we appreciate." The thanks might also appear in the parent newsletter or in a parent postcard written by a child or teacher. You know something like that will probably end up right on the refrigerator door, too.

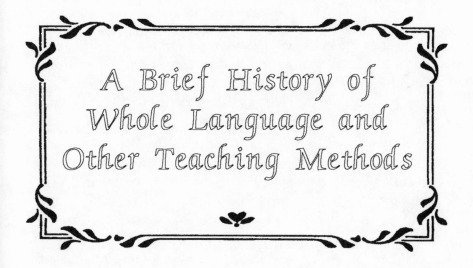

A Brief History of
Whole Language and
Other Teaching Methods

When I first began teaching, I used the techniques I had been taught in my teacher education courses in college. I did my best to teach children phonics using basal readers, and to make sure that each student learned to spell each word correctly. The children learned to write by copying, rather than expressing their own thoughts, and any errors were circled in red so that the children could focus on what they were doing wrong.

Each year, I ended up having three different reading groups in my classroom. There were the top students who learned quickly and grew bored just as fast. Good readers usually find it easier to win in school, but I was introducing a letter a week to the class, and the good readers had to work on the letter even if they already knew it. To be truthful, I was ignoring these children, and they knew that, too.

Then there was the middle group that muddled through as best they could, doing what had to be done. They learned bits and pieces -- like "s" for snake -- but creativity, excitement and curiosity were not expected or encouraged.

Unfortunately, there was also the "young" or the "slow" or the "bottom" group, which was comprised of children who were not really ready for pencil and paper work. They did the best they could, but the teaching methods and materials simply did not work for them. By the end of the school year, many of them had started acting out and were on their way to remedial reading classes, where they would learn more bits and pieces, to the extent they learned anything at all. Others simply withdrew, and they were the hardest to work with because they tried so hard to be invisible. I tried hard to help them, even if they wanted me to ignore them, but most of them still ended up with poor grades and negative attitudes in my class and in the years that followed.

I've learned to forgive myself for what I did to those children, but I now believe this process hurt many students. I was trying to force young children to adapt to a rigid system, and when it didn't work, the children were rejected rather than the system. Fortunately, teachers across America are now rejecting the system rather than the children, utilizing instead a Whole Language approach which supports each child's natural inclination to learn and lets every child win in the classroom every day.

The Origins of Whole Language

The Whole Language approach originated in New Zealand, and while some Americans might assume that the U.S. has little to learn from a small, remote country like New Zealand, recent United Nations statistics show that New Zealand has the highest literacy rate in the world. The U.S., in comparison, ranks at the bottom of 19 industrialized nations in reading, writing and arithmetic.

The origins of Whole Language in New Zealand are also significant because they grew out of attempts to help bilingual minority students whose parents had migrated to the cities. In New Zealand, the minority students were the islands' original inhabitants -- known as Maoris -- whose native language is a Polynesian dialect.

According to *The Foundations of Literacy* by Don Holdaway, one of the originators of Whole Language in New Zealand and a wonderful author and speaker, "the generative ideas included a determination to apply genuine developmental principles to the problem (and a willingness to research such principles); the enrichment of a basic language-experience methodology by the enjoyment of a rich literature in story, chart, and song; techniques required to bring such a rich, open literature into the competence of young, uninitiated learners; and a frontal attack on the problem of competition and other aversion-producing influences within the school environment."

Marie Clay was another important figure in the growth of Whole Language. She did developmental research on learning to read and write, and her work emphasized the importance of teachers' monitoring and responding to children's attempts to learn. She also found that children tend to teach and correct themselves when placed in a supportive environment.

A third influential figure was Sylvia Ashton-Warner, a teacher in New Zealand. She worked in a rural Maori school, and according to Don Holdaway, "her insight was that reading should be motivated by the deepest springs of meaning in the human heart." She focused her students on words that were meaningful to them, and she also used an integrated curriclum (the combining of various subject areas) to reinforce the learning of reading and writing and to make the process more relevent.

By combining these techniques, teachers in New Zealand were able to teach bilingual and English-speaking children to read and write more effectively. And, the children developed more positive attitudes about reading, writing, school in general, and themselves.

The success of the Whole Language approach in New Zealand resulted in its spreading to Australia, England, Canada and other parts of the British Commonwealth. In 1975, an official committee in Britain issued a report entitled "A Language for Life," which called for changes throughout the education system based on what was known about the relationships between language, thinking and learning. This report supported the Whole Language approach and led to its adoption by an increasing number of schools.

In particular, the Whole Language appoach has become standard practice in parts of Canada. Even in the provence of Quebec, which has a substantial French-speaking population, an offical policy statement of the Ministry of Education mandates a "whole-language, child-centered, integrated approach."

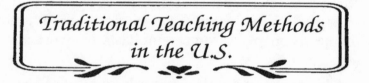

Traditional Teaching Methods in the U.S.

American teachers have tried a variety of different teaching methods during the twentieth century, and the question of which one is "best" has been a source of ongoing, bitter debate.

The **Language Experience** approach was popular prior to 1920, again in the late 1920s and early 1930s, and yet again in the late 1960s and early 1970s. Its emphasis was on helping children use their own experiences to establish meaning through their work with print, while the teacher used the children's words to teach skills. Roach Van Allen, one of its proponents, explained it simply by saying "Anything I can say, I can write; anything I can write, I can read."

The **Phonics** approach was also popular from the start of the century into the 1920s, and again in more recent times. According to this method, reading equals the meaning derived from certain combinations of letters. Children therefore "sound out" words by learning the sounds associated with specific letters. Unlike the Language Experience approach, the phonics approach placed greater emphasis on the words themselves than on their meaning to the children.

From the 1930s to the mid-1960s, the **Sight Word** approach replaced the Phonics approach in many schools. The focus of this approach was on recognizing entire words, in the belief that the more words children can recognize, the more they can read. Like Phonics, this approach places more emphasis on words than meaning.

A **Linguistic** view of language learning also became popular during the 1950s and the 1960s. This approach emphasized the recognition of spelling patterns, in part through the use of examples such as "Nan can fan Dan." Children were expected to internalize patterns of spelling, based on their correspondence to sounds. And, like the Phonics and Sight Word approaches, the Linguistic approach focused children on the words rather than their meaning.

Basal readers, which combined elements of the Phonics, Sight Word, and Linguistic approaches, became popular during the late 1950s. Academic experts and publishers worked together to create fundamental reading programs that provided massive guidance for teachers (such as manuals and resource books), combined with illustrated books for children. For example, a basal reader would include a picture of a white dog with black spots on it, and the accompanying text would read "See Spot. See Spot run."

While the variety of word-oriented approaches described above were being used, new work was being done with meaning-oriented approaches as well. Grace Fernald pioneered the use of tactile and kinesthetic techniques, in which children worked with hands-on objects and acted out stories, instead of working solely with abstract symbols such as letters and words. Jeanette Veatch introduced developmental reading strategies which included the use of trade books that children could choose for themselves and read at their own pace.

As advocates of word-oriented and meaning-oriented teaching strategies continued to debate the merits of their approaches, an attempt was made in 1967 to settle the matter once and for all. Jeanne Chall's *Learning To Read: The Great Debate* examined research on both approaches and concluded that the word-oriented Phonics approach worked best. This influential work led to more emphasis on "decoding" text in books and workbooks, as well as the inclusion of word analysis questions in achievement tests.

However, other studies, including one commissioned by the U.S. Office of Education, questionned Chall's conclusions. In addition, an article entitled *Debunking The Great Phonics Myth*, by Marie Carbo, summarized a variety of problems with Chall's research and the teaching methods resulting from it. Chall herself, in an article entitled "Learning To Read: The Great Debate 20 Years Later," states "Indeed, it has been common practice in our Reading Laboratory at Harvard to have beginning readers learn the alphabetic principle, read the best of children's literature, and write stories and messages -- all designed to foster a love of reading and books." While continuing to maintain that that a word-oriented approach works better, Chall also noted that teaching phonics alone, isolated from literature, was not the recommendation of *The Great Debate*.

As concern increased about illiteracy and poor reading and writing skills in the U.S., a national commission was appointed to look into the issue. Its report, *Becoming A Nation Of Readers*, defined reading as "a process of extracting meaning from written texts." It went on to say that students spend far too little time reading and too much time doing workbook and skill sheet exercises in school. Members of the commission called for the development of new reading tests that would assess deeper levels of reading comprehension, rather than focusing on word recognition.

An editorial by Robert Cole in Phi Delta Kappan magazine also helped to put the issue in perspective when it stated "For too long the field of reading has been characterized by turf wars and plagued by the request for one right answer. It is time to lay to rest the old territorial battles, and to move decisively in the direction of helping our students learn to read well."

Whole Language in the U.S.

At about the time *The Great Debate* was published, a small band of educators were starting to develop the techniques and philosophy which would lead to the spread of the Whole Language movement in America. Ken Goodman, who later became president of the International Reading Association, and Yetta Goodman were particularly influential in regard to reading instruction, while Donald Graves had a profound impact on the teaching of writing.

One of the key tenets of the movement they helped start was a resistance to the influence of prescribed instructional programs and standardized tests on the curriculum. Rather than gearing teaching methods to such publications, the Whole Language pioneers turned their attention to the experiences of the children they were teaching. Their philosophy was that all children could become literate if they were treated with support and respect, and if the classroom environment promoted the sharing of written language in a meaningful way.

Ken Goodman, Yetta Goodman, and other educators with a similiar point of view became early members of a non-profit organization called the Center for the Expansion of Language and Thinking, which helped them develop widespread support for their approach. As teachers across the U.S. began learning about Whole Language, as well as trying it in their classrooms and seeing how well it worked, they began forming their own local TAWL (Teachers Applying Whole Language) groups. And, as educational publishers became aware of the growing popularity of Whole Language, they began racing to produce Whole Language books and classroom materials instead of basal readers and other phonics-based publications.

While many people have contributed to the success of the Whole Language movement in the U.S., it has primarily been a result of teachers working on a grassroots level, doing the best they can to help children learn to read and write. My own evolution as a Whole Language teacher during the last decade may provide a helpful perspective on this process.

In the late 1970s, I was a readiness teacher in New Hampshire, providing an extra year of supportive learning experiences for developmentally young 6 year-olds. Around 1978, I began using Mary Baratta-Lorton's *Mathematics Their Way*, which helps make mathematics understandable to young children through the use of hands-on materials. The success of this process-oriented approach clearly showed me the benefits of adjusting the curriculum to the needs of the children, instead of trying to make the children adjust to the curriculum.

I was introduced to the writing process around 1980. We were very lucky to have Donald Graves in New Hampshire at that time, and his work helped me and many other teachers provide more opportunities for children to write in school. In the mid-1980s, the New Hampshire Association of Readiness Teachers sponsored a week-long workshop with Don Holdaway, and this experience provided me with my first in-depth exposure to the Whole Language approach.

Throughout these years, the teaching techniques I used in the classroom were evolving, much as I was. Learning to use the Whole Language approach is a process, similar in many ways to learning to read and write. It cannot be learned in a single workshop or in-service. Events such as these provide a philosophical framework and many helpful suggestions, but a full understanding of Whole Language teaching methods can only be attained by working with students in the classroom year after year, and reflecting on that experience.

Now that I have started leading Whole Language workshops, teachers sometimes come up to me after a session and say they have always used a Whole Language approach, even if it might not have been called that. This may be true, but I believe we all need to continue to grow as teachers -- by attending workshops and conferences, by collaborating with other professionals, and by learning from our students. Like our students and ourselves, the Whole Language approach will continue to evolve in our classrooms, if we let it.

Also like students, educators need to feel safe in order to take the risks needed for growth. Part of my job as a workshop leader and consultant is to help teachers try new approaches that will enable them to provide a more effective learning environment for their students. This process works far better when we heed Robert Cole's advice and focus on what happens in the classroom, not who's right and who's wrong.

It takes a lot of energy to oppose someone else, and people who are in opposition have difficulty maintaining an effective working relationship. I have learned that Whole Language is the right approach for me and the children I work with, but I understand that other teachers may feel differently. Rather than insisting that my way is the right way, I choose to demonstrate to other educators what works in my classroom, and then let them make their own decisions.

I encourage those who have questions about Whole Language, or who disagree with it, to visit a Whole Language classroom and experience the process for themselves. Plan a time to talk to the teacher and the students, and then go through the same process in a classroom where skills, workbooks, and basal readers are emphasized.

Afterwards, think about yourself and how you learn, and how you've taught young children to walk and talk or read and write. You have to do what you believe is right, and finding out what that is is part of the process.

Resources

Teachers' Bibliography

Atwell, Nancie. *In The Middle*. Portsmouth, NH: Heinemann, 1987.

Baratta-Lorton, Mary. *Mathematics Their Way*. Reading, MA: Addison-Wesley.

Baskwill, Jane and Paulette Whitman. *Whole Language Source Book*. Toronto: Scholastic Tab, 1988.

Baskwill, Jane and Paulette Whitman. *Evaluation: Whole Language, Whole Child*. Toronto: Scholastic Tab, 1988.

Beaton, Clare. *Costumes*. New York: Warwick Press, 1990.

Calkins, Lucy. *The Art of Teaching Writing*. Portsmouth, NH: Heinemann, 1986.

Clay, Marie M. *Observing Young Readers*. Portsmouth, NH: Heinemann, 1982.

Clay, Marie M. *What Did I Write?* Portsmouth, NH: Heinemann, 1975.

Clay, Marie M. *The Early Detection of Reading Difficulties*. Portsmouth, NH: Heinemann, 1985.

Clay, Marie M. *"Concepts About Print" Tests*. Portsmouth, NH: Heinemann.

Cochrane, Orin, et al. *Reading, Writing, and Caring*. New York: Richard C. Owen Publishers, 1984.

Cranfield, Jack and Harold Wells. *100 Ways to Enhance Self-Concept in the Classroom*. Englewood Cliffs, NJ: Prentice-Hall.

Doake, David. *Reading Begins at Birth*. Toronto: Scholastic Tab, 1988.

Gentry, J. Richard. *Spel...Is A Four-Letter Word*. Portsmouth, NH: Heinemann.

Goodman, Kenneth, et al. *What's Whole in Whole Language*. Portsmouth, NH: Heinemann, 1986.

Goodman, Kenneth, et al. *Language and Thinking In School: A Whole-Language Curriculum*. New York: Richard C. Owen Publishers, 1987.

Goodman, Kenneth, et al. *The Whole Language Evaluation Book*. Portsmouth, NH: Heinemann, 1989.

Goodman, Kenneth, et al. *Whole Language Catalog*. Santa Rosa, CA: American School Publishers, 1991.

Graves, Donald. *Writing: Teachers and Children at Work*. Portsmouth, NH: Heinemann, 1983.

Graves, Donald and Virginia Stuart. *Write From the Start*. Portsmouth, NH: Heinemann.

Hansen, Jane. *Breaking Ground: Teachers Relate Reading and Writing in the Elementary School*. Portsmouth, NH: Heinemann, 1985.

Harste, Jerome, et al. *Language Stories and Literacy Lessons*. Portsmouth, NH: Heinemann, 1985.

Harste, Jerome and Kathy Short. *Creating Classrooms for Authors*. Portsmouth, NH: Heinemann, 1988.

Hart, Leslie. *Human Brain and Human Learning*. Brain Age Publishers.

Holdaway, Donald. *The Foundations of Literacy*. New York: Scholastic, 1979.

Holdaway, Donald. *Stability and Change in Literacy Learning*. New York: Scholastic.

Holdaway, Donald. *Independence in Reading*. New York: Scholastic, 1980.

Irvine, Joan. *How To Make Pop-Ups*. Winnipeg, MAN: Blue Frog Books.

Newman, Judith. *The Craft of Children's Writing*. Portsmouth, NH: Heinemann, 1984.

Newman, Judith (Ed.). *Whole Language: Translating Theory Into Use*. Portsmouth, NH: Heinemann, 1985.

Routman, Regie. *Transitions -- From Literature to Literacy*. Portsmouth, NH: Heinemann, 1988.

Smith, Frank. *Understanding Reading*. New York: Holt, Reinhart & Winston.

Smith, Frank. *Insult to Intelligence*. Portsmouth, NH: Heinemann, 1986.

Trelease, Jim. *The Read-Aloud Handbook*. New York: Penguin Books.

Wittels, Harriet. *How To Spell It Dictionary*. New York: Grosset and Dunlap.

Children's Books

A (BB) following a book means it is a Big Book.
A (P) following a book means it can also be used as a play which the students perform.

Ahlberg, Janet & Allen. *The Jolly Postman*. Boston: Little Brown & Co., 1986.

Allen, Pamela. *Who Sank The Boat*. Crystal Lake, IL: Rigby. (BB) (P)

Anderson, Hans Christian. *The Little Match Girl*. New York: G.P. Putnam & Co., 1987.

Asch, Frank. *Mooncake*. New York: Scholastic, 1983. (BB)

Asch, Frank. *Bread and Honey*. New York: Parents Magazine Press, 1981.

Babcovich, Lydia. *Busy Beavers*. New York: Scholastic. (BB)

Barrett, Judi. *Animals Should Definitely Not Wear Clothing*. New York: Aladdin, 1970. (P)

Barret, Judi. *Old MacDonald Had An Apartment House*. New York: Aladdin, 1969.

Bate, Lucy. *Little Rabbit's Loose Tooth*. New York: Crown Publishers Inc., 1975.

Bemelmans, Ludwig. *Madeline*. New York: Scholastic, 1989. (BB)

Berenstein, Stan & Jan. *The Spooky Old Tree*. New York: Random House Inc., 1987. (P)

Berenstein, Stan & Jan. **Bears In The Night**. New York: Random House, 1971.

Bonne, Rose. **I Know A Lady.** New York: Puffin, 1984. (P)

Borden, Louise. **Caps, Hats, Socks and Mittens**. New York: Scholastic. (BB)

Bradford, Annie North. **Frosty the Snowman**. New York: Golden Press, 1972. (P)

Branlen, Franklin. **Big Tracks, Little Tracks**. New York: Scholastic, 1960.

Branlen, Franklin. **The Moon Seems To Change**. New York: Harper & Row, 1963.

Branlen, Franklin. **What The Moon Is Like**. New York: Harper & Row, 1961.

Brown, Marcia. **Stone Soup**. New York: Aladdin Books, 1947. (BB) (P)

Brown, Margaret Wise. **The Golden Egg Book**. New York: Golden Press, 1971.

Brown, Margaret Wise. **The Important Book**. New York: Harper & Row, 1949.

Browne, Anthony. **Piggy Book**. New York: Alfred A. Knopf, 1986. (P)

Burrows, Peggy. **The Enchanted Book**. New York: Rand McNally & Co.

Chernoff, Goldie Taub. **Puppet Party**. New York: Scholastic, 1971.

Cohen, Miriam. *Best Friends*. New York: Aladdin Books, 1971.

Cohen, Miriam. *Will I Have A Friend?* New York: Aladdin Books, 1967.

Cole, Joanna. *Boney Legs*. New York: Scholastic, 1983.

Cowley, Joy. *Hairy Bear*. San Deigo: The Wright Group. (BB) (P)

Cowley, Joy. *Mrs. Wishy-Washy*. San Diego: The Wright Group. (BB) (P)

Cowley, Joy. *The Farm Concert*. San Diego: The Wright Group. (BB) (P)

Cummings, E.E. *Little Tree*. New York: Crown Publishers, 1923.

Dabcovich, Lydia. *Busy Beavers*. New York: Scholastic. (BB)

DePaola, Tomie. *Pancakes For Breakfast*. New York: Harcourt, Brace Jovanovich, 1978.

DePaola, Tomie. *The Legend of The Blue Bonnet*. New York: G.P. Putman's Sons, 1983.

DePaola, Tomie. *Charlie Needs A Cloak*. Englewood Cliffs, NJ: Prentice-Hall, 1973.

DePaola, Tomie. *The Cloud Book*. New York: Scholastic, 1975.

Fleischman, Paul. *Joyful Noise.* New York: Harper & Row, 1988.

Frost, Robert. *Birches*. New York: Henry Holt & Co., 1988.

Galdone, Paul. *The Three Billy Goats Gruff*. Dayton, OH: Clarion, 1973. (P)

Greenfield, Eloise. *Day Dreamers*. New York: Dial Books, 1981.

Greenfield, Eloise. *Honey, I Love.* New York: Harper & Row, 1972.

Grimm, Jacob & Wilhelm. *Little Red Riding Hood*. New York: Scholastic, 1971. (P)

Goffsten, M.B. *A Writer*. New York: Harper & Row, 1984.

Hague, Kathleen. *Bear Hugs*. New York: Henry Holt & Co., 1989.

Hall, Donald. *Ox-Cart Man*. New York: Puffin Books, 1979. (BB) (P)

Hallinan, P.K. *That's What A Friend Is*. Nashville, TN: Ideals Pub. Corp.

Hazen, Barbara. *The Gorilla Did It*. New York: Aladdin, 1974.

Hazen, Barbara Shook. *Rudolph The Red Nosed Reindeer*. New York: Western Pub. Co., 1958. (P)

Heine, Helme. *Friends*. New York: Aladdin Books, 1986.

Holabird, Katharine. *Angelina and The Princess*. New York: Clarkson N. Potter, Inc., 1984.

Hoberman, Mary Ann. *A House Is A House For Me*. New York: Scholastic, 1978. (BB)

Hackaday, Hal. *Don't Be The Leaf*. Allen, TX: DLM. (BB)

Howe, James. *I Wish I Were A Butterfly*. New York: Harcourt Brace Jovanovich, 1987. (P)

Howe, James. *There's A Monster Under My Bed*. New York: Atheneum, 1986.

Humphrey, Margo. *The River That Gave Gifts*. New York: Childrens Book Press, 1987.

Jorgensen, Gail. *Crocodile Beat*. Crystal Lake, IL: Rigby. (BB)

Joseph, Lynn. *Coconut Kind Of Day*. New York: Lothrop, Lee & Shepard Books, 1990.

Kent, Jack. *The Catarpiller and the Polliwog*. Englewood Cliffs, NJ: Prentice-Hall, 1982.

Krauss, Ruth. *The Carrot Seed*. New York: Scholastic. (BB)

Larrick, Nancy. *When The Dark Comes Dancing*. New York: Philomel Books, 1983.

Lindbergh, Reeve. *The Midnight Farm*. New York: Dial, 1987.

Lionni, Leo. *Tico and the Golden Wings*. New York: Alfred A. Knopf, 1964.

Lottridge, Celia. *One Watermelon Seed*. Oxford: Oxford Press, 1986.

Martin, Bill Jr. *Brown Bear, Brown Bear What Do You See?* New York: Holt, Rinehart, and Winston, 1967. (BB) (P)

Martin, Bill Jr. *I Am Freedom's Child*. Allen, TX: DLM. (BB)

Martin, Bill Jr. *Knots On A Counting Rope*. New York: Holt, Rinehart & Winston, 1987.

Mathews, Greda Bradley. *What Was That!* New York: Western Publishing Co., 1977.

Mathews, Greda Bradley. *Bunches and Bunches of Bunnies*. New York: Scholastic, 1985. (BB)

Mayer, Mercer. *Merry Christmas Mom and Dad*. New York: Golden Press. (P)

Mayer, Mercer. *Just For You*. New York: Golden Press, 1975.

Mayer, Mercer. *Just Me and My Dad*. New York: Golden Press, 1977.

Mayer, Mercer. *There's A Nightmare In My Closet*. New York: Dial Press, 1968.

McQueen, Lucinda. *The Little Red Hen*. New York: Scholastic, 1985. (BB) (P)

Morgan, Pierre. *The Turnip*. New York: Philomel Books, 1938. (P)

Numeroff, Laura. *If You Give A Mouse A Cookie*. New York: Scholastic, 1985. (BB) (P)

North, Carol. *The Gingerbread Man*. New York: Golden Books, 1981. (P)

Orback, Ruth. *Apple Pigs*. New York: Philomel Books, 1976.

Ormerod, Jan. *Sunshine*. New York: Puffin Books, 1981.

O'Toole, Mary. *A Strange Visitor*. Cleveland: Modern Curriculum Press. (BB)

Parker, Nancy Winslow & Joan Richards Wright. *Bugs*. New York: Mulberry Books, 1987.

Parkes, Brenda & Judith Smith. *The Gingerbread Man*. Crystal Lake, IL: Rigby. (BB) (P)

Parkes, Brenda & Judith Smith. *The Three Billy Goats Gruff*. Crystal Lake, IL: Rigby. (BB) (P)

Parkes, Brenda. *Who's In The Shed*. Crystal Lake, IL: Rigby. (BB)

Potter, Beatrix. *The Tale of Peter Rabbit*. New York: Alfred A. Knopf, 1986.

Prelutsky, Jack. *The Random House Book of Poetry*. New York: Random House, 1983.

Rohmer, Harriet & Mary Anchondo. *How We Came To The Fifth World*. New York: Children's Book Press, 1976.

Ryder, Joanne. *Catching The Wind*. New York: Morrow Junior Books, 1989.

Rylant, Cynthia. *When I Was Young In The Mountains*. New York: E.P. Dutton, 1982.

Sendak, Maurice. *Chicken Soup With Rice*. New York: Scholastic. (BB) (P)

Shaw, Charles. *It Looked Like Spilt Milk*. New York: Harper & Row, 1947.

Silverstein, Shel. *Where The Sidewalk Ends*. New York: Harper & Row, 1974.

Silverstein, Shel. *The Giving Tree*. New York: Harper & Row, 1964.

Slobodkina, Esphyr. *Caps For Sale*. New York: Scholastic, 1940. (BB) (P)

Stevenson, Robert Louis. *My Shadow*. New York: David R. Godine, 1989.

Stinson, Kathy. *Red Is Best*. Toronto: Annick Press Ltd., 1982. (P)

Tarrant, Graham. *Honeybees*. New York: G.P. Putnam's Sons, 1984.

Tarrant, Graham. *Rabbits*. New York: G.P. Putnam's Sons, 1984.

Tarrant, Graham. *Butterflies*. New York: Putnam, 1983.

Tudor, Tasha. *A Time To Keep*. New York: Rand McNally & Co., 1977.

Turner, Ann. *Nettie's Trip South*. New York: Scholastic, 1987.

Udry, Janice May. *A Tree Is Nice*. New York: Harper & Row, 1956.

Van Allsberg, Chris. *The Polar Express*. Boston: Houghton Mifflin, 1986.

Velthuijs, Max. *Frog In Love*. New York: Farrar Straus Giroux, 1989. (P)

Viorst, Judith. *Alexander and the Terrible Horrible No Good, Very Bad Day*. New York: Aladdin, 1972.

Wagner, Jenny & John Brown. *Rose and the Midnight Cat*. New York: Puffin, 1977.

Weir, Alison. *Peter, Good Night*. New York: Dutton, 1989.

Welber, Robert. *The Winter Picnic*. New York: Knopf/Pantheon, 1973.

Wells, Rosemary. *Noisy Nora*. New York: Scholastic, 1973. (BB)

Wells, Rosemary. *Benjamin & Tulip*. New York: Dial Press, 1973.

Werner, Jane. *Cinderella*. New York: Golden Press, 1982. (P)

Werner, Jane. *Snow White*. New York: Golden Press, 1973. (P)

Wexler, Jerome. *Flowers Fruits and Seeds*. Englewood Cliffs, NJ: Prentice-Hall, 1987.

Wiesner, David. *Free Fall*. Dayton, OH: Lothrop, Lee, & Shepard, 1988.

Wildsmith, Brian. *Cat On A Mat*. Oxford: Oxford University Press, 1982.

Wildsmith, Brian. *All Fall Down*. Oxford: Oxford University Press, 1983.

Wildsmith, Brian. *Squirrels*. Oxford: Oxford University Press, 1974.

Wilhelm, Hans. *I'll Always Love You*. New York: Crown Publishing, 1985.

Yagawa, Sumiko. *The Crane Wife*. New York: Mulberry Books, 1979. (P)

Yolen, Jane. *Owl Moon*. New York: Philomel Books, 1987.

Young, Miriam. *Jellybeans for Breakfast*. New York: Random House, 1968.

Zimmermann, Werner H. *Henny Penny*. New York: Scholastic, 1989. (BB) (P)

Zolotow, Charlotte. *I Know A Lady*. New York: Puffin, 1984. (P)

Records, Tapes & Other Classroom Materials

Music

Amidon, Peter & Mary Alice. Brattleboro, VT.

Chapin, Tom. New York, NY: Sundance Music.

Charette, Rick. N. Windham, ME: Pine Point Records.

Grammar, Red. Peekskill, NY: Smilin' Atcha Music.

Greg & Steve. Los Angeles, CA: Youngheart Records.

Harley, Bill. Seekong, MA: Round River Records.

Houston, Whitney. *Greatest Love of All*. New York: Arista Records.

Our Dinosaur Friends. Covina, CA: American Teaching Aids Inc.

Palmer, Hap. Freeport, NY: Educational Activities Inc.

Raffi. Willowdale, ONT: Troubadour Records.

Rosenshontz. Brattleboro, VT: RS Records.

Sharon, Lois & Bram. Toronto, ONT: Elephant Records.

Wee Sing. Los Angeles, CA: Price Stern Sloan, Inc.

Recorded Stories

Bodkin, Odds. Bradford, NH: The Wisdom Tree.

Hayes, Joe. *Coyote and Native American Folk Tales*. Santa Fe, NM: Trails West Publishing.

Lane, Marcia. *Tales on the Wind*. Albany, NY: Stories and Songs for Children.

O' Callahan, Jay. W. Tisbury, MA: Vineyard Video Productions.

Simms, Laura. *Laura Simms Tells Stories Just Right For Kids*. Toronto, ONT: Kids Records.

Classroom Materials

Blocks:
Dr. Drew's Blocks
Boston, MA

Chart Paper or Sentence Strips:
New England Supply
Springfield, MA

Chart Paper or Sentence Strips:
J.L. Hammett Company
Braintree, MA

Magnetic Boards:
The Magnetic Way
Getzville, NY

Nature Books, Films & Magazines:
National Wildlife Federation
Washington, DC

Personal Spelling Guides for Students:
Modern Learning Press
Rosemont, NJ

Pocket Charts:
The Wright Group
San Diego, CA

Record Keeping Charts:
American Teaching Aids
Covina, CA

Spiral Binding:
General Binding Corporation
Northbrook, IL

Writing Trays:
Childcraft
Edison, NJ

Classroom Equipment List

General

Tables & chairs
Bookshelves which display book's front covers
Storage buckets for each child (I use wash tubs)
Cozy/rocking chair
Pillows
Stuffed animals
Rug area
Easels for displaying big books (Make sure the part of the easel that the books will rest on is flat, not upturned, so the pages will turn easily.)
Mirror
Flannel board & stories
Magnetic boards
Flag
Bulletin boards
Calendar

Reading Center

Picture books
Story books
Non-fiction books
Big books
Magazines
Nursery rhymes
Plays
Poetry
1 box of lined chart paper
Mimeograph paper (for making small books)
Reading folder for each child
Tapes for recording each child's reading
Sentence strips & holder
Puppets and puppet theatre

Writing Center

Trays or storage tubs for each child
Pre-sharpened pencils
Scented markers (I teach children not to "fill in" with the markers -- just outline -- so they'll last)
Crayons
Mimeograph paper
Colored manila paper (for covers of published books)
1" binding tape
Typewriter or computer
Parent assistance (to make books)
Staples and stapler
Spiral binding machine

Math Center

Mathematics Their Way book
Blocks
Teddy bear and dinosaur counters
Unifix cubes
Geo boards
Kidney beans (one side spray painted)
Pattern blocks
Junk boxes
Tiles
Wooden cubes
Scales
Large graphing plastic
Jewels
Geometric shapes
Cuisenaire rods
Folder for each child

Science Center

Publications including Peterson Guides, National Geographic books & filmstrips, Your Big Back Yard or Ranger Rick magazines, Audobon Society books, etc.
Seashells
Rocks
Fossils
Plants
Magnets
Clocks/timers
Measuring tape
Thermometer
Terrarium
Aquarium
Magnifying glass
Seeds, soil & potting containers
Plastic models of animals
Folder for each child

Art Center

18" x 24" paper for making big books, or roll of paper
2" masking tape for binding
1" masking tape for binding
2" cloth tape
Glue sticks (large)
Doilies
Glitter
Cotton balls
Clay (modeling)
Tissue paper
Paper plates
Construction paper
Paint (mixed) & brushes
Crayons
Scissors

Paste
Glue
Watercolors
Staplers
Adhesive tape
Large rolls of paper
Tongue depressors

Listening Center

Piano, autoharp or other instruments
Record player and/or tape recorder with microphone
Records and/or tapes -- music, recorded stories, musicals
and plays, etc.

Play Area

Mail box
Blocks
Rubber farm animals, dinosaurs and people
Wooden road signs for block area
Playhouse area
Dolls
Sand & water tables (black concrete mixing tubs are inexpensive and work great)
Woodworking bench (ask a parent to keep it filled with wood)
Tools
Mathematics Their Way supplies
Globe
Doll house furniture
Hats & other clothing
Cardboard rolls from inside paper towels and wrapping paper
Strawberry mesh baskets
Popsicle sticks
Tops from jars and bottles
Boxes

Notes